THE VIRTUOSO GUITARIST
Method for Guitar

VOLUME 1

A New Approach To Fast Scales

MATT PALMER

ISBN 978-0-615-47465-6

Copyright © 2008, 2011 Matt Palmer. International copyright secured. All rights reserved. The unauthorized use, distribution, reproduction or copying of this work without prior written permission of the copyright holder is strictly forbidden. Any unauthorized use of this work or any part herein is subject to international copyright law.

Photography by Mamta Popat, Tucson, AZ

Visit Matt Palmer online at www.mattpalmerguitar.com

mp Music Co.

Dedication

To my beautiful wife Gladys
for all your love and support.

Acknowledgements

I would like to express my sincere gratitude to the many people who have provided assistance and inspiration to me in the creation of this work. To my primary instructors, Dr. William Yelverton, Dr. Richard Todd, Dr. Douglas James, Dr. Donald Hamann, and Professor Thomas Patterson for encouraging the further development of this technique. To David Russell, Sergio Assad, and Odair Assad for the lessons, encouragement, and inspiration. To Marc and Debbie Sandroff, David Francis, Phyllis and Sandy Bolton, Dennis and Sevren Coon, Don and Carol Eagle, Ralph Grosswald, and Bill Wolfe for your friendship and support. To Schott Music GmbH & Co KG, European American Music Distributors LLC, and Bèrben Edizioni Musicali for kindly granting permissions to use musical excerpts. To Christy Shivell, Jesse James Mazzoccoli, João Paulo Figueirôa, David Francis, Mamta Popat, and Carlos Rodriguez Quirós for your invaluable comments and feedback. To all my friends and fans for your enthusiastic interest in the technique. Finally to my wife, Gladys, for believing in me always. Without your support none of this would have been possible.

Contents

Foreword	9
History of Development	10
Key to Notation	12
Part I: The Left Hand	
Initial Thoughts on Left-Hand Fingerings	15
Efficiency and Ease of Execution	16
Part II: The Right Hand	
Fundamental Approach	21
Consistency of Tone	22
Rest Stoke vs. Free Stroke	24
One Event	24
The Triplet Problem	25
Strings With Two Notes	27
Beginning the Ascending Scale	28
Beginning the Descending Scale	30
Musical Application 1	31
Part III: Advanced Applications	
Introduction	35
Changing Direction	36
Musical Application 2	42
Chromatic Scales and Complex Figures	43
Musical Application 3	46
The Ascending Shift	48
The Descending Shift	56
Shifting on a Single String	59
Musical Application 4	61
Closing Remarks	63
Scales Reference	65
About the Author	81

Foreword

This text provides a unique approach to playing fast scales on the guitar. I have developed this technique during my years as a classical guitarist, and have enjoyed much success in applying it to the repertoire of the guitar. The technique is an organized, yet highly flexible system of playing scales with three fingers of the right hand, as opposed to the traditional two. The primary focus of this method is on the problems of the right hand when playing scales with three fingers. However, by necessity, the approach to left-hand fingerings is also unique – inspired by various disciplines in the art of guitar. The thorough study and mastery of this method will enable guitarists to play scales at faster tempos using a fraction of the effort normally required to do so. Furthermore, this organized system will simplify the process of fingering scale passages. The ultimate goal of this method is to eliminate the technical difficulties of performing fast scales, thus allowing performers to focus more upon musicianship.

It should be noted here that it is not my intention to disregard the teachings of the old masters. This method is intended to supplement traditional techniques, rather than replace them. In fact, at times this technique relies heavily upon a thorough mastery of the techniques pioneered in the past. This method provides an alternative means of performing *very fast* scales. Traditional techniques should be adequate for use in passages at moderate tempos. However, due to the inherent efficiency of this method, guitarists may also find these techniques valuable as a means of conserving energy in large-scale works or within the course of a concert performance.

The techniques presented in this method are intended for intermediate and advanced guitarists. A thorough knowledge of classical guitar technique is assumed. Both hands must be adequately trained to play advanced techniques. If pain or discomfort occurs, stop immediately to rest and evaluate the situation. Overexertion and/or playing material beyond one's current ability can lead to injury. Beginners working from this method should do so under the guidance of an experienced instructor. Guitarists of all disciplines can benefit from the study of this method, provided they possess a basic knowledge of standard notation and an understanding of the mechanics of the right hand.

Various methods of executing scales are presented throughout the course of this work to prepare readers for musical application of A-M-I scale technique. The advanced applications demonstrate how the technique can be applied to a wide variety of situations. However, the countless variations and permutations of scales that exist in music far exceed the scope of this text. This method will give readers the fundamental tools to be able to shape the technique to their specific needs. These fundamentals are the unset foundations of the technique, a flexible set of formulas and techniques ready to be shaped and molded to support musical applications.

History of Development

The development of this technique relates directly to my development as a guitarist. My early studies were focused entirely upon the electric guitar. I was inspired by amazing guitarists such as Jason Becker, Paul Gilbert, Yngwie Malmsteen, Marty Friedman, and John Petrucci, among others. These men all had an ability to play solos with incredible speed. I studied this music for over 10 years as a youth. Though I am now a classical guitarist – and no longer play this style of music – I attribute much of my ability and understanding of the fretboard to these musicians.

When I began studying classical guitar at age 20, my hands were clearly out of balance. My left hand was quite agile and fast, but my right-hand fingers were severely underdeveloped. This discrepancy was so discouraging that I nearly quit the classical guitar. Thankfully, I took encouragement from my success with tremolo technique, which I worked on early in my classical studies. After working many hours on this technique, I found it to be quite effortless. The sequence P-A-M-I is certainly one of the most efficient and natural ways of moving the fingers of the hand (which is why in classical repertoire we find so many tremolo works exceeding five minutes). The speed at which I could play tremolo gave me hope that I might someday be capable of playing virtuosic repertoire without a guitar pick.

Like most young guitar students, the music I was studying was far beyond my capabilities at the time. In my first year of classical guitar studies, I was working on advanced pieces by Giuliani, Tárrega, and Villa-Lobos, among others. One obvious technical flaw was my inability to play fast scales. I did work diligently on the technique of alternating I-M to play scales, and was showing much improvement. However, after some time I began to feel as if my right hand would never be able to match the speed of my left. It seemed that to do so would require me to develop and master a different right-hand scale technique.

The basic ingredients of my technique were always right in front of me, but, as so often happens with a new concept, they were difficult to recognize. I suppose my left-hand ideas were what ultimately led me to a solution. Due to my past as an electric guitarist, I was often in disagreement with editors when it came to fingering scales within a piece. One traditional left-hand technique of playing scales that is prevalent in editions throughout the classical repertoire is what I call "in the box" technique, or position playing. This technique is demonstrated perfectly with Andres Segovia's fingering of the 2-octave C major scale.

Segovia's 2-octave C major scale

With this fingering, we are required to play the scale in two distinct positions – 2nd position and 5th position. The fingering is such that all the notes fall easily "in the box" of four frets, each finger of the left hand responsible for its own respective fret. Completing the scale requires a shift from the 2nd position to the 5th position on the third (G) string, where the second octave of the scale is completed.

Scales such as this are important lessons in shifting and navigating the fretboard, and certainly deserve attention in the practice room. However, in performance situations, particularly those that require a swift execution of scales, such fingerings are less than favorable. A valuable lesson I learned from playing the electric guitar was how to play scales at great speed with the utmost efficiency. That efficiency comes from arranging scales in three-note per string patterns. In contrast, below is an alternate fingering of the same scale.

2-octave C major scale (three notes per string)

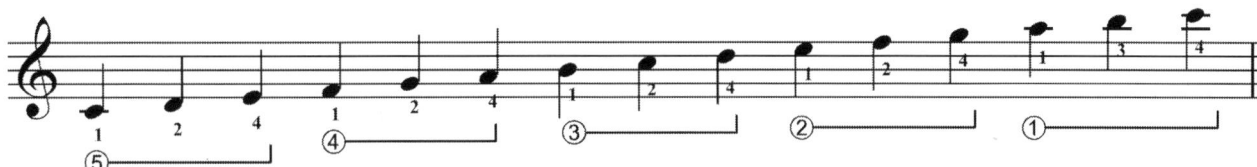

This fingering eliminates the risky and laborious three-position shift on the 3rd string, replacing it with what I call a "half shift" on the 4th to 3rd string crossing and a simple one-fret shift on the 3rd to 2nd string crossing. Furthermore, and just as important, the left hand is basically doing the same thing on every string, making this type of fingering easier both mentally and physically.

Though not an entirely new concept on the classical guitar, three-note per string scales were a major factor in the development of this technique. It became clear that the logical solution to my problem was to arrange scales three notes per string and employ a three-finger right-hand technique to complement this arrangement. Given my past success at tremolo technique, I decided after experimentation that A-M-I was the most efficient solution. It is a simple idea, and one that I have since developed into more complex patterns that allow its use in a wide variety of situations.

Key to Notation

Right-hand fingers are represented by the letters P-I-M-A.

    P – Thumb

    I – Index

    M – Middle

    A – Ring

Left-hand fingers are represented by the numbers 1-2-3-4.

    1 – Index

    2 – Middle

    3 – Ring

    4 – Pinky

Strings on the guitar are represented by circled numbers.

    ① – E (high)

    ② – B

    ③ – G

    ④ – D

    ⑤ – A

    ⑥ – E (low)

A bracket indicates how many notes are played on each string.

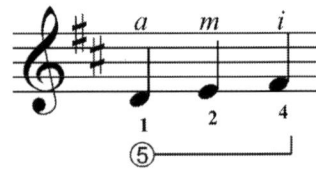

In the example above, all three notes are played on the 5th string, as indicated by the bracket.

Part I
The Left Hand

Initial Thoughts on Left-Hand Fingerings

One at a Time

When playing scales on the guitar, the most efficient way to use the fingers is one at a time. In most cases, after a finger is used it should be returned to its relaxed state (off the fretboard). Doing so eases tension in the left hand, which allows greater possibilities of speed and stamina. Furthermore, this practice leaves the finger prepared for its next use.

Finger 2 or Finger 3?

An excellent question is whether to use fingers 1-2-4 or fingers 1-3-4 when executing a succession of two whole steps on the same string. Answers to this question would vary greatly in the guitar world. Two arguments will be made here for the use of finger 2 in most situations.

1. It is easier to stretch finger 2 away from finger 1 than it is to stretch finger 4 from finger 3. To test this, place finger 1 on the 3rd fret of the guitar and reach to the 5th fret with finger 2. Now, place finger 3 on the 3rd fret and reach to the 5th fret with finger 4. Which is easier?
2. The three-note per string method of fingering scales requires frequent one-fret shifts and half shifts. The benefits of using finger 2 for the initial whole step can best be seen when ascending a three-note per string scale. When ascending the scale and approaching a shift or half shift, the natural tendency of finger 1 is to pull closer to finger 2 after fingers 2 and 4 have depressed their respective frets. This places finger 1 in a better position to make such a shift or half shift. Conversely, when using finger 3 for the initial whole step the tendency of finger 1 is to stay back around the fret it just depressed.

Though not an integral aspect of this method, this is the rationale behind the left-hand fingerings found in the notation. For the reasons mentioned above, I encourage you to consider finger 2 for most occasions. However, on the upper registers of the guitar (above the 12th position) I find it more comfortable to use finger 3 in this situation. I find that the awkward position in which we are required to place our left hand to execute passages above the 12th fret, coupled with the fact that the frets are positioned closer together in the highest registers of the guitar, makes the use of finger 2 a difficult task, particularly for those with larger, longer fingers.

Efficiency and Ease of Execution

One problem with "in the box" left-hand technique is the fact that awkward shifts need to be made to reach notes in higher registers.

Figure 1.1

Figure 1.1: C major scale – as fingered by Andres Segovia

The scale above only spans two octaves, and yet with this type of fingering we are required to execute a three-fret shift in order to reach the position of the second octave. Though a valuable lesson in shifting and fretboard navigation, this fingering offers little in regards to efficiency. Furthermore, this fingering lacks a certain ease of execution that leads to greater mental and physical effort, which results in insecurity and, ultimately, mistakes.

A much more efficient way of executing the same scale is to arrange the scale in three-note per string patterns.

Figure 1.2

Figure 1.2: ascending three-note per string scale

This fingering allows for a much greater ease of execution. The action on each string can be thought of as a progression from finger 1 to finger 4, or the reverse in a descending scale. The inner note is most often going to be depressed by finger 2, except in instances of a whole step followed by a half step (in this scale, the fingering on the E string), in which case finger 3 is used. In effect, we are making the same basic movement on every string. Furthermore, the difficult three-fret shift is eliminated with this fingering. Replacing this shift is a simple one-fret shift on the 3rd to 2nd string crossing, and a "half shift" on the 4th to 3rd string crossing.

A half shift is a shift that does not require a repositioning of the left-hand thumb. This occurs in certain circumstances when finger 4 is depressed on the same fret of two adjacent strings, and a whole step is found at the string crossing, as shown in the figures below.

Figure 1.3

Figure 1.3: ascending half shift

Figure 1.4

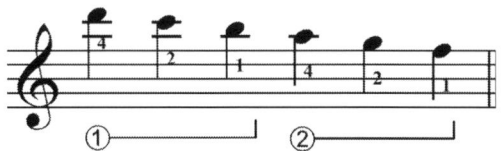

Figure 1.4: descending half shift

The movement of finger 1, though technically putting the left hand in a different position, requires a minimum amount of effort to reach one fret beyond its previous position. This type of shift does not require any movement of the supporting thumb. Therefore, the movement of the left hand can be isolated to the movement of finger 1.

By maintaining an ease of execution with regard to the movements of the left hand, the physical and mental effort required to perform scale passages is greatly reduced. Arranging scales three notes per string limits the frequency, distance, and difficulty of shifts necessary to reach notes in higher registers, and furthermore allows us to maintain consistent and easy motions with the left hand. These ideas lead to a greater potential for speed and efficiency.

Part II
The Right Hand

Fundamental Approach

The fundamental approach to this scale technique is quite simple. Pitches from a particular scale are arranged in three-note per string patterns, and the right hand repeats the fingering A-M-I. The sequence of attacks in the right hand is of the utmost importance. The sequence A-M-I follows the principles of sympathetic motion, much like the natural closing of the hand. It is therefore a naturally efficient way of moving the hand – similar to tremolo technique. This direction of motion towards the thumb is also consistent with the ease of execution idea discussed in Part I. The mastery of this technique can easily provide guitarists with a simple and effective method of playing scales on the guitar. Efficiency and ease of execution are key factors in the fluid and effortless technique required to play scales at great speed.

The figure below demonstrates the basic approach to A-M-I scale technique over an ascending C major scale.

Figure 2.1

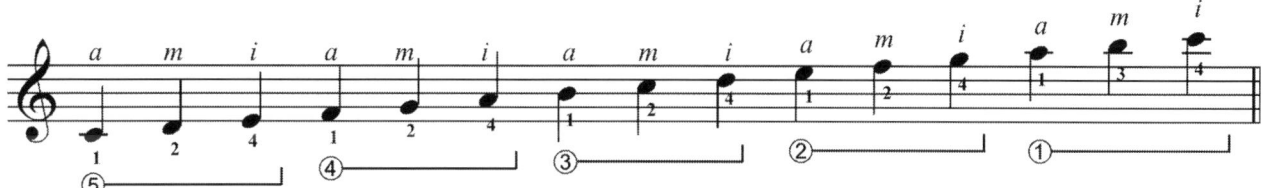

Figure 2.1: ascending C major scale

Observe in this C major scale how each string begins with an attack of the A finger. Furthermore, the attack of the A finger consistently coincides with the use of left-hand finger 1, while the attack of the I finger is with finger 4. In the descending scale, a similar consistency can be found. The attack of the A finger now coincides with the use of left-hand finger 4, while the I finger is with finger 1.

Figure 2.2

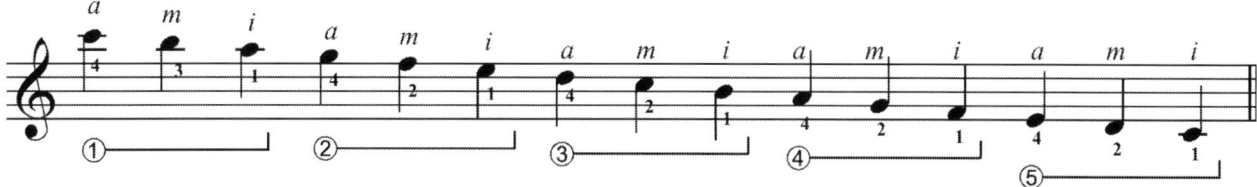

Figure 2.2: descending C major scale

* IMPORTANT * As can be seen upon further study of this method, when playing scales that proceed stepwise I am always in pursuit of fingerings that allow me to maintain the consistencies found in the figures above. No matter the events that occur within the course of a scale – direction changes, shifts, strings with more or less than 3 notes on them, etc. – I always attempt to maintain or immediately return to the idea of three-note per string scales attacked with A-M-I. This adds a great deal of consistency to the method, and makes the process of fingering and executing these events much easier. Furthermore, as you will see in the advanced application of the technique, the vast amount of fingering possibilities that usually exists is replaced with a relatively small number of formulas that can be applied to various scenarios.

Consistency of Tone

It is necessary to approach this technique with a keen ear to tone production. Due to a variety of factors, including finger length, nail shape, and finger strength, our tone can vary from finger to finger. Most guitarists have developed a consistent attack between the I and M fingers due to a highly developed I-M scale technique. However, it is quite common to find inconsistencies of tone when the A finger is added to the equation. Attentive practice must be exercised to alleviate this problem. Many methods for doing so exist, and I encourage you to recall those lessons that you previously used. However, I will outline my approach to developing a consistent tone in the following passages.

First, choose your favorite finger; the finger with the tone you wish to emulate. Attack your open E string repeatedly with this finger, paying close attention to all the subtle aspects of the sound, including volume, color, fullness, and attack sound.

The next step is to reproduce this tone perfectly with a different finger. I prefer to begin by reproducing the percussive aspect of the attack. Every well-placed attack has a characteristic percussive sound accompanying it. Perhaps you have worked diligently to alleviate this sound, but due to the nature of our instrument it will always be there. A means of muting the strings may be useful in this exercise. Push through the string to reproduce this sound, referring back to your favorite finger to serve your memory if necessary.

Once the percussive side of the attack has been reproduced, a perfect consistency of tone is now within reach. To match the color of the previous finger, you may need to slightly adjust the angle of attack on the string. A slight reshaping of the nail may also be necessary. Be aware of the initial plant of your finger on the string and observe closely how the string reacts to the weight of your plant. Also, watch with great attention the motion of the string as you push through and release it. Repeat the above steps with each finger, along with any other methods you may know, to achieve a consistent tone between A-M-I.

I have had much success with practicing different finger combinations when playing scales. Try alternating I-M, A-M, and I-A in addition to A-M-I in your scale practice routine. By doing so, you are developing a consistent tone, as well as strengthening the relationship between the fingers.

The following exercise can be used to develop a consistent sound from the fingers of the right hand. By attacking the open E string multiple times with the same finger, we create a consistent tone that can be matched by the other fingers. This process allows our ears a greater opportunity to discern slight variances in tone that may be overlooked using other methods.

Exercise 2.1

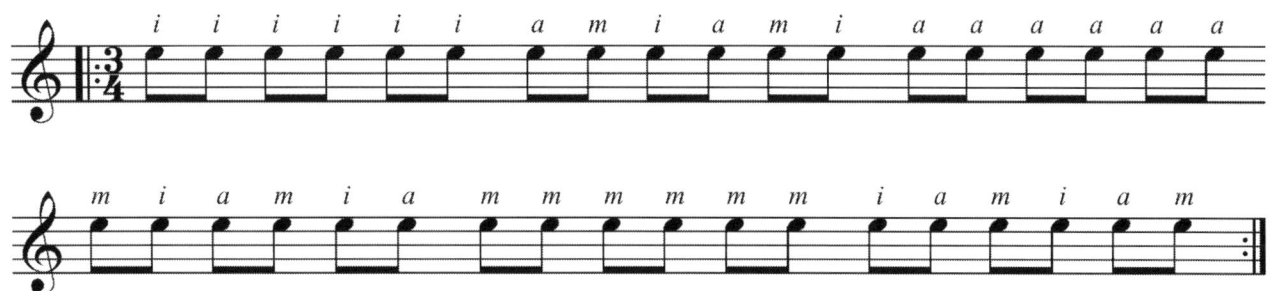

Exercise 2.1: tone-matching exercise

This simple exercise should also be repeated over fretted notes, as the attack of the right hand has a slightly different feel compared to the open strings.

Another useful exercise for developing a consistent tone with A-M-I is to play scales with repeated notes. In the following exercise, each note is attacked twice and the scale is arranged three notes per string. As a result, we still have the same string crossing with the A finger. There are a total of six attacks per string (A-M-I-A-M-I).

Exercise 2.2

Exercise 2.2: tone-matching exercise with repeated notes

Try the above scale with four attacks per note as well. The ideal string crossing with the A finger remains intact. Some simple math can also lead you to other useful exercises with repeated notes.

Rest Stroke vs. Free Stroke

My preference for playing fast scales is to use a stroke somewhere between a free stroke and a rest stroke (a "frest" stroke?). I generally do not alter the angle of my wrist in relation to the strings to achieve a rest stroke sound. I have worked hard to make my free stroke sound like a rest stroke, while keeping the hand and wrist in position. My follow-through *does* touch the string below like a rest stroke does. However, I do not commit the weight to the follow-through of the attack to produce the rest stroke sound. In contrast, I commit the weight to the plant and to the attack itself. This method seems to allow my fingers to recuperate and return to their starting positions faster. Try both methods of attack to achieve a level of comfort that suits you, and the sound quality that you desire. I suggest starting with a relatively light attack as you get used to the motions required to play evenly. Once you have achieved evenness, gradually increase the power of your strokes.

One Event

When I play fast scales – or anything fast for that matter – I try to simplify things mentally and physically. Instead of viewing a passage as 16, 24, or however many notes, I view these notes as one "event." This has had an incredible impact upon my performance and interpretative abilities. A-M-I scales are perfect for explaining this, because the idea applies physically as well as mentally. To demonstrate, gently make a fist with your right hand, starting with the pinky and ending with the index finger. With a smooth motion, this can easily be felt as one event. Do the same with only A-M-I. Try the same thing with the left hand. Now try with left-hand fingers 4-2-1 or 4-3-1. Coordinate both hands on the guitar with this idea and you are producing three notes with only one stroke of effort.

Once you master the one event idea, try to apply it to large-scale passages as well. Performing one event is much easier than playing 24 notes. This idea also adds a great deal of interest and artistic integrity to the interpretation of fast scales or flurries of notes in music. After all, I like to imagine that great composers do not write *scales* – only events or gestures that happen to be comprised of scales.

The Triplet Problem

Several aspects of this technique contribute to the danger of having all scale passages sound like triplets. This is great if you *are* playing triplets, but an absolute disaster if you are not. In an extended passage of 16th notes in four-note groupings, the finger attacking on the strong beats varies cyclically. I overcame this problem by giving heavy accents to the strong beats, and focusing roughly 75% of my A-M-I scale practice upon exercises of 16th notes in four-note groupings. Due to the nature of the technique – three-note per string scales being attacked by three fingers of the right hand – triplets come quite naturally and should therefore require significantly less practice to master.

Exercise 2.3

Exercise 2.3: accent exercise

Interestingly, the accents in such passages follow the sequence A-M-I.

The following exercises contain single-string passages that are designed to help with the triplet problem. Always obey the accents on the beats. These simple four-note figures can also make nice additions to your daily warm-up routine.

Exercise 2.4

Exercise 2.4: accent exercise

Exercise 2.5

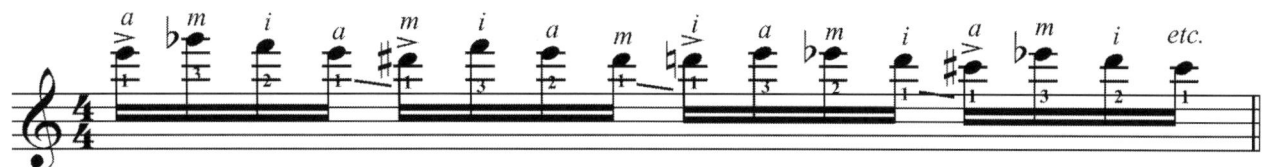

Exercise 2.5: single-string chromatic exercise

Continue the above pattern all the way down to the open string. Many other four-note patterns may assist you as well. Experiment with others you may know.

The following exercise demonstrates the same basic principle presented above, only this time within the course of a 2-octave D major scale.

Exercise 2.6

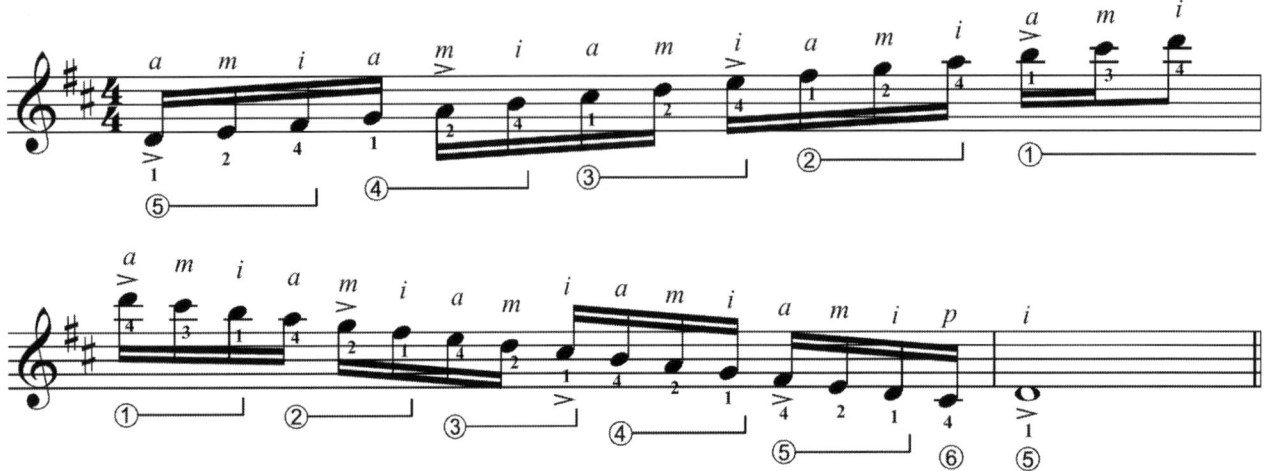

Exercise 2.6: accent exercise in D major

It is also useful to arrange three-note patterns into four-note groupings, as shown below.

Exercise 2.7

Exercise 2.7: accent exercise for three-note patterns

Strings With Two Notes

It is impossible to consistently maintain three-note per string patterns in musical applications. The most common occurrence is the placement of two notes on a string. Though somewhat inconvenient, it is actually quite easy to overcome this problem. Our first priority is to keep a similar motion with our right hand. This can be achieved by playing two-note strings with M-I. In this fashion, we are still moving towards the thumb.

Figure 2.3

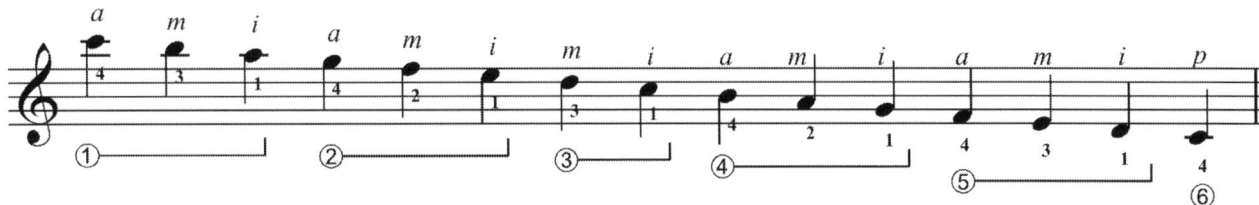

Figure 2.3: descending scale with two notes on the 3rd string

A similar fingering is used when ascending.

Figure 2.4

Figure 2.4: ascending scale with two notes on the 2nd string

These solutions demand a strong M-I scale technique, particularly when you are playing at great speed. As can be seen in the figures above, there is an M-I-M-I alternation on the transition between the 2nd and 3rd strings. This happens frequently using this method, so keep that technique strong! We will discuss other solutions to this problem in our shifting and alternate string crossing exercises later. Notice the use of P at the end of Figure 2.3. This is a comfortable way to end a scale of this type, if the musical context allows. It is also a great way to change direction and begin an ascending scale, which is the topic of a later section.

Beginning the Ascending Scale

There are several options for beginning the ascending scale. All solutions provided here work quite well. However, the option you ultimately choose to use will be based upon the context of the music you are performing. A goal of this technique is to provide a certain consistency that prevails under any musical situation. As shown in the previous sections, the preferred sequence of fingering fast scales with the right hand is A-M-I. It would therefore be ideal to retain this motion towards the thumb if we are to be consistent with our technique.

The first option is simply to begin with three notes on the initial string and use the right-hand fingering A-M-I, as discussed previously.

Figure 2.5

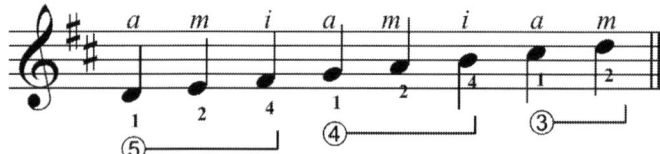

Figure 2.5: beginning the ascending scale with three notes on the initial string

Next, there is the option of beginning with two notes on the initial string. In this case, the ideal fingering to initiate the scale is M-I. This technique maintains our desired ease of execution, as we are still keeping the motion of the right hand moving towards the thumb.

Figure 2.6

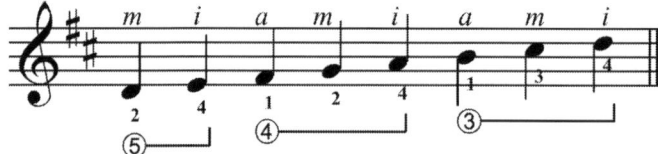

Figure 2.6: beginning the ascending scale with two notes on the initial string

A very effective way of beginning an ascending scale with two notes on the initial string is to begin the scale with a slur. By using a slur, we can set the tempo with the left hand alone, rather than demanding the same from both hands at once. We can initiate the slur with either the thumb or the index finger. If given the choice, I would use the thumb, as this makes the first four attacks of the right hand a tremolo-like technique.

Figure 2.7

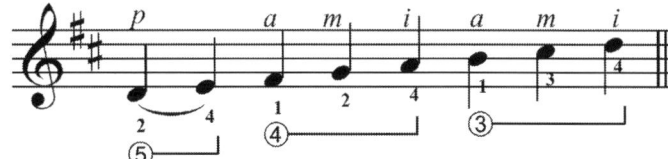

Figure 2.7: beginning the ascending scale with the thumb and a 2-4 slur

Beginning this same scale with the index finger also has its advantages. This is the same fingering used when beginning a descending scale with a slur (as shown in Figure 2.13). Another benefit of this technique is that the thumb is free to attack a bass note, if needed.

Figure 2.8

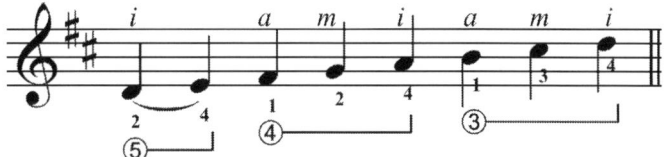

Figure 2.8: beginning the ascending scale with the index finger and a 2-4 slur

The next option is to begin the scale with one note on the initial string. In this case, we also have the option of starting with the thumb or index finger.

Figure 2.9

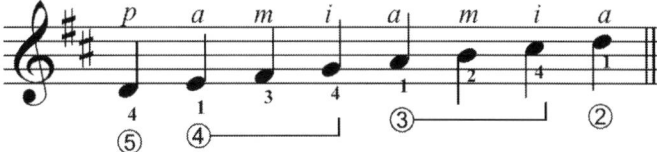

Figure 2.9: beginning the ascending scale with one note on the initial string

Figure 2.10

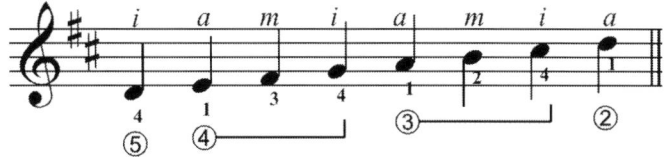

Figure 2.10: another option of beginning the ascending scale with one note on the initial string

Beginning the Descending Scale

When beginning the descending scale, we have options available to us that are similar in concept to those of the ascending scale. The most ideal options are starting the scale with one, two, or three notes on the initial string. The use of the thumb is not an effective option when initiating a descending scale, as this action forces the right hand into an awkward position.

Figure 2.11

Figure 2.11: beginning the descending scale with three notes on the initial string

Figure 2.12

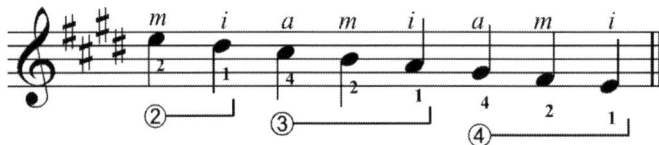

Figure 2.12: beginning the descending scale with two notes on the initial string

Figure 2.13

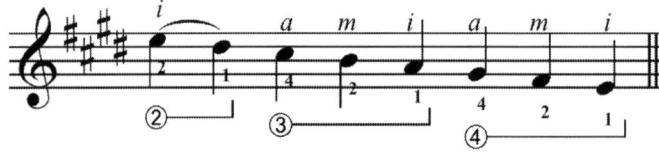

Figure 2.13: beginning the descending scale with two notes on the initial string and a 2-1 slur

Figure 2.14

Figure 2.14: beginning the descending scale with one note on the initial string

Musical Application 1

Example 2-1. Ástor Piazzolla, Tango Suite for 2 guitars, II. *Andante*

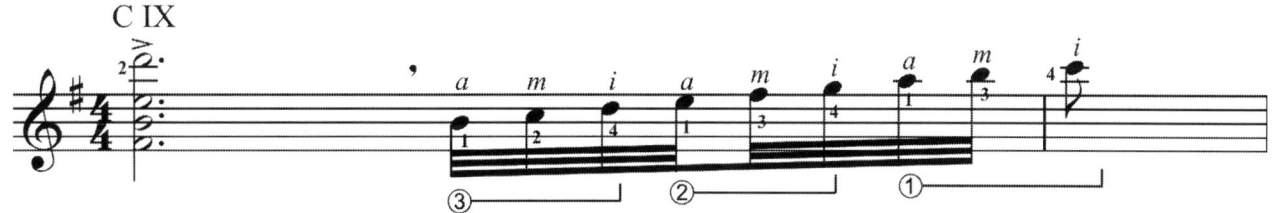

© 1987 Bèrben Edizioni Musicali, Ancona – Italy. All rights reserved. Used by permission.

Example 2-2. Mauro Giuliani, *Rossiniana* Op. 119

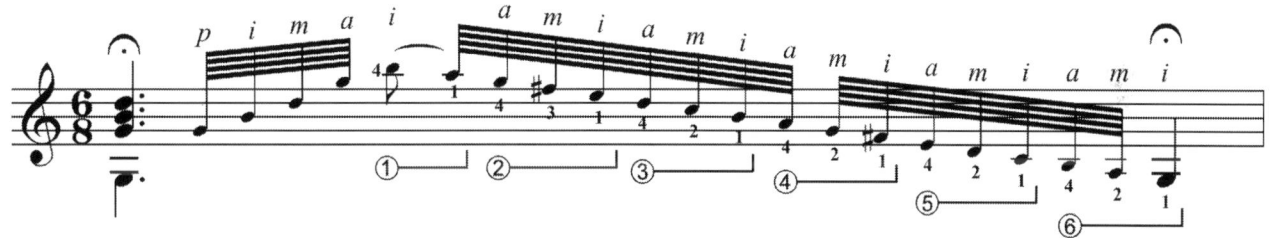

Example 2-3. Luigi Legnani, Caprice No. 7

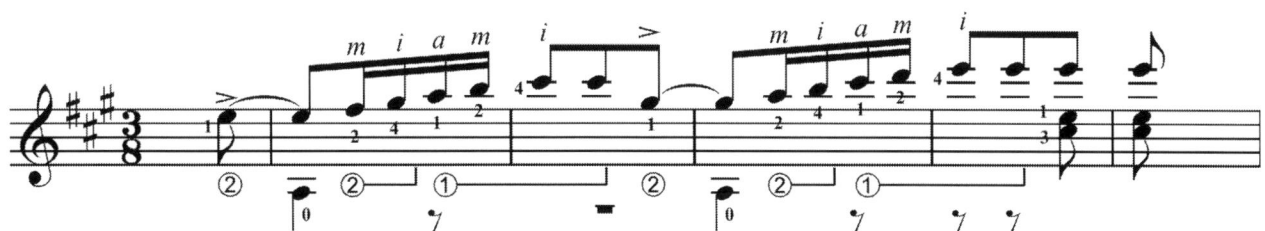

Example 2-4. J.S. Bach, *Chaconne* from Partita in D minor BWV 1004

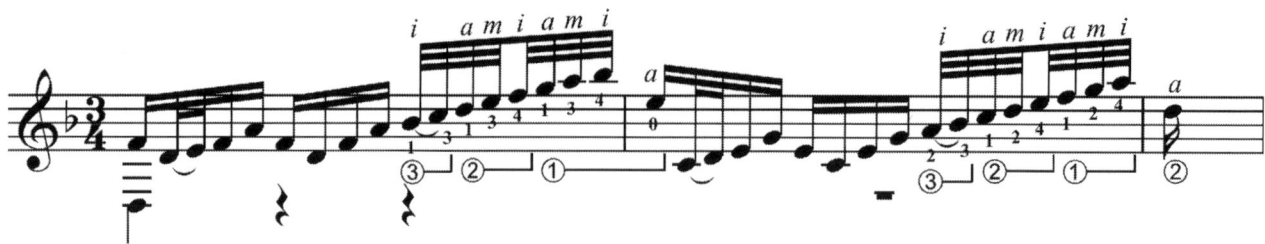

Example 2-5. Fernando Sor, Variations on a Theme of Mozart Op. 9

Example 2-6. Mauro Giuliani, *Gran Sonata Eroica* Op. 150

Example 2-7. Mauro Giuliani, *Gran Sonata Eroica* Op. 150 (alternate fingering)

Part III

Advanced Applications

Introduction

Now that you have been introduced to the basic fundamentals of A-M-I scale technique, we need to move on to specific problems that you will inevitably come across in musical contexts. In a perfect world, all scales within a piece of music could be arranged three notes per string, and scales would never change direction, skip intervals, require shifts, etcetera. However, in reality these things do happen – frequently. So how do we deal with these circumstances that interrupt our consistent and methodical approach to playing scales? We need to develop consistent and methodical solutions that can be applied to a wide variety of special circumstances. This chapter deals with these special problems, including:

- Changing direction (the "turnaround")
- Chromatic scales and complex patterns
- Use of the thumb
- Alternate string crossings
- Shifting

The techniques presented in this chapter build upon the fundamentals of A-M-I scale technique discussed previously. Musical applications may require the simultaneous use of two or more of these techniques. If you find it difficult to make these fingerings work in your application, consider alternate left-hand fingerings. In my experience, a brief "sacrifice" of difficulty in the left hand can often lead to a much more manageable passage or section of music.

Changing Direction - The "Turnaround"

Changing direction in a scale can give rise to several technical problems. This section deals with these problems and presents several unique solutions to them. For the most part, these solutions allow us to continue with the principles we have established and avoid unusual right-hand string crossings. For the need of a noun to describe the act of changing direction, I have dubbed these techniques "turnarounds." Each turnaround is named after how many notes are on the string where the change of direction occurs.

The most basic turnaround we can execute is one that does not interfere with our repetition of A-M-I. As one might assume, this turnaround has three notes on the string that the change of direction occurs.

Figure 3.1

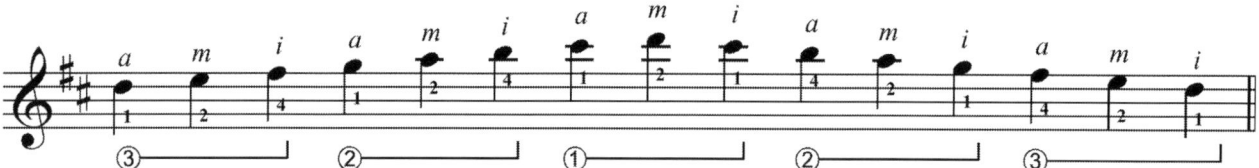

Figure 3.1: ascending scale with a 3-note turnaround

Figure 3.2

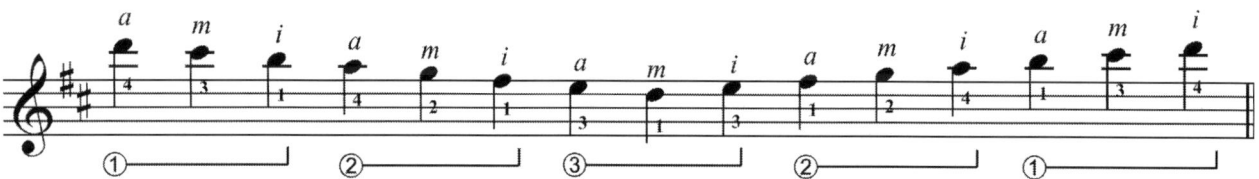

Figure 3.2: descending scale with a 3-note turnaround

In our next turnaround, a shift is executed on a single string, producing six total notes on that string. Thus, we have two repetitions of A-M-I on a single string in this type of turnaround. This keeps the A-M-I pattern unbroken, and is very useful if you need to finish a scale in a higher position than you started.

Figure 3.3

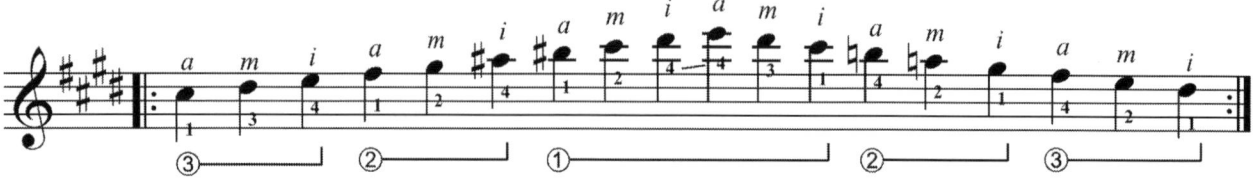

Figure 3.3: ascending scale with a 6-note turnaround

If you perform the repeat found in the figure above, you will execute another 6-note turnaround. This turnaround is the reverse of our initial 6-note turnaround, as demonstrated in the figure below.

Figure 3.4

Figure 3.4: descending scale with a 6-note turnaround

The next figure contains yet another 6-note turnaround option. This technique is useful when we need to arrive in a lower position than we started.

Figure 3.5

Figure 3.5: variation of the 6-note turnaround

The turnaround shown above may be more effective when the shift is only a half step. There is also the possibility of executing this type of turnaround with finger 1 instead of finger 4, as shown below.

Figure 3.6

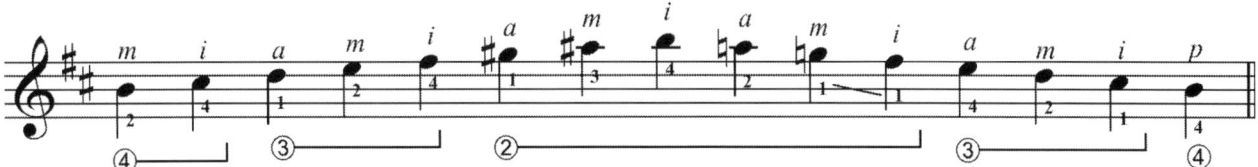

Figure 3.6: another variation of the 6-note turnaround

Another turnaround we can use is a 5-note pattern on a single string. For this type, there are two valid possibilities for our right-hand fingering: M-I-A-M-I or A-M-I-M-I. In the grand scheme of things, these are virtually the same pattern if we approach the turnaround with A-M-I and continue afterwards with A-M-I. However, the pattern I prefer is M-I-A-M-I. The reason is: when there are instances of only two notes on a string, we *begin* that string with M-I. Therefore, to maintain a more consistent technique I chose to *begin* the 5-note turnaround with M-I as well. Do consider both, as each hand is different. Interpretation may at times influence your decision between the fingering options above.

Figure 3.7

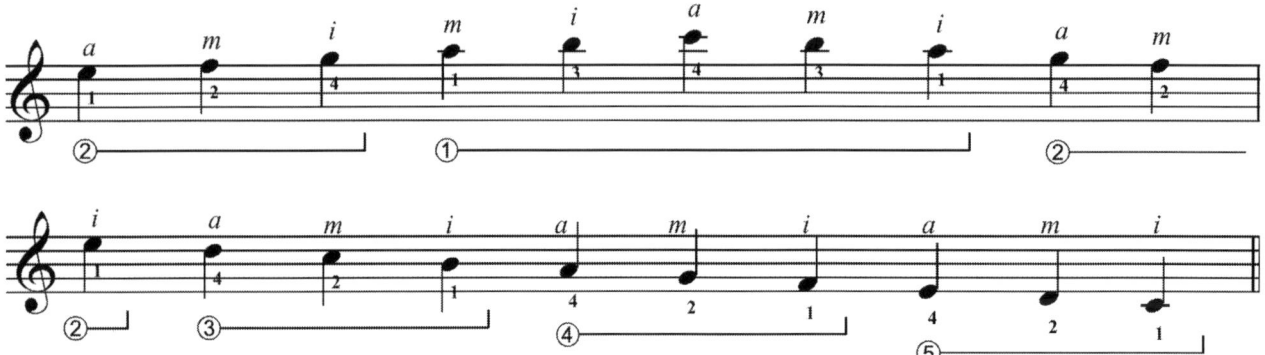

Figure 3.7: the 5-note turnaround

Figure 3.8

Figure 3.8: 5-note turnaround in opposite direction

The next turnaround we have in our arsenal makes use of the thumb. This turnaround is useful when the music consists of a descending scale followed by an ascending scale. In this case, the attack of the thumb is on the lowest note of the scale and is the only note on the string.

Figure 3.9

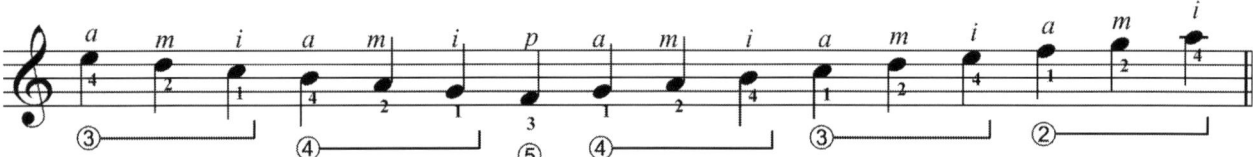

Figure 3.9: 1-note turnaround with use of the thumb

The following figure uses the thumb to execute the turnaround as well. However, in this case the attack of P is followed by a slur. This requires us to shift to the next position of the scale. There are more desirable ways to play this scale, but in a musical context your possibilities may be limited. It is also possible to use M-I in place of the slur.

Figure 3.10

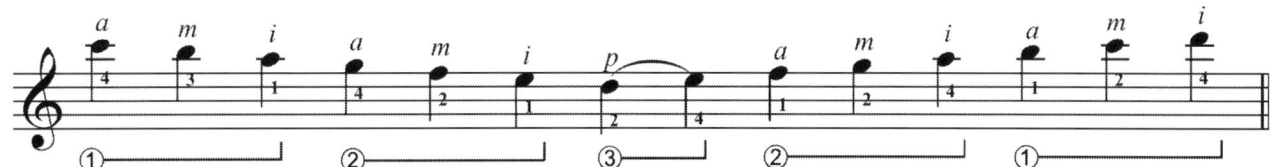

Figure 3.10: 2-note turnaround with the use of the thumb and a slur (change of position)

Try the following exercises as you practice changing direction in scales. Exercise 3.1 contains uses of the 3-note and 6-note turnarounds. The continual string crossings in Exercise 3.2 give it a multi-purpose training role.

Exercise 3.1

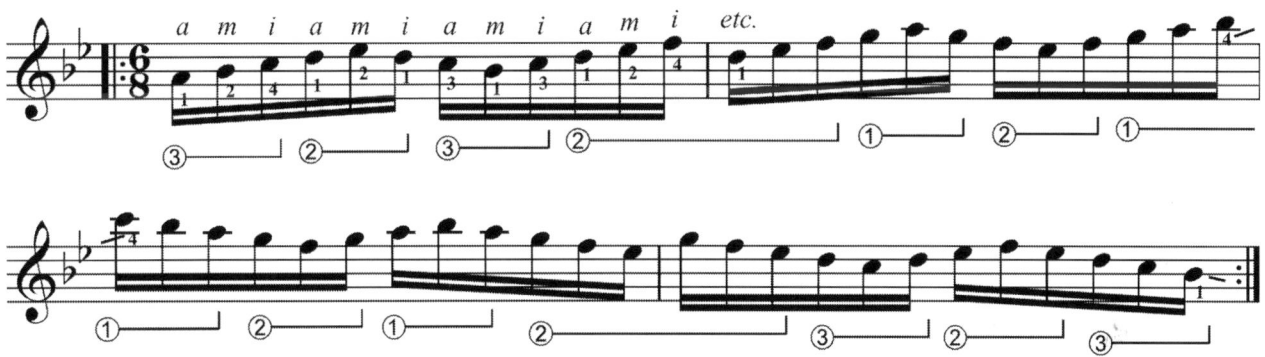

Exercise 3.1: changing direction

Exercise 3.2

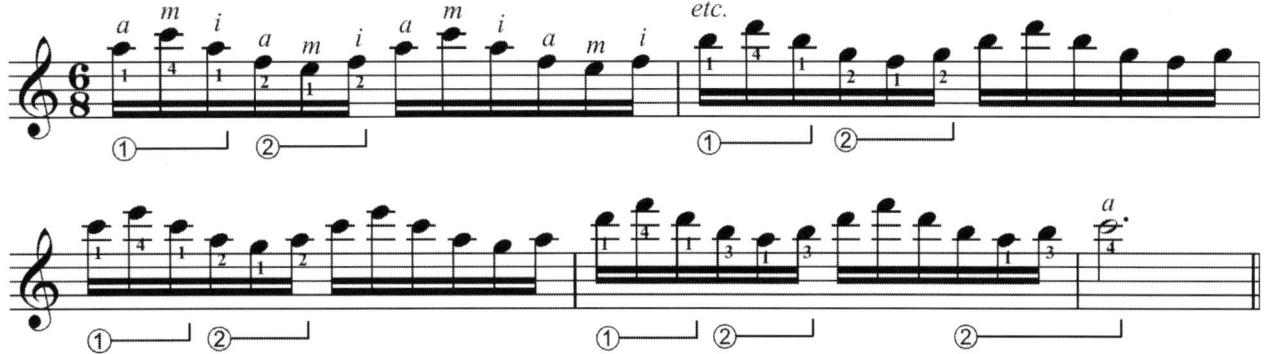

Exercise 3.2: changing direction

When a change of direction occurs at the outset of a scale (i.e. right at the beginning), a few more fingering sequences are possible. The first possibility is the 4-note turnaround. This turnaround often requires a change of position, but may be the most efficient possibility in certain musical contexts.

Figure 3.11

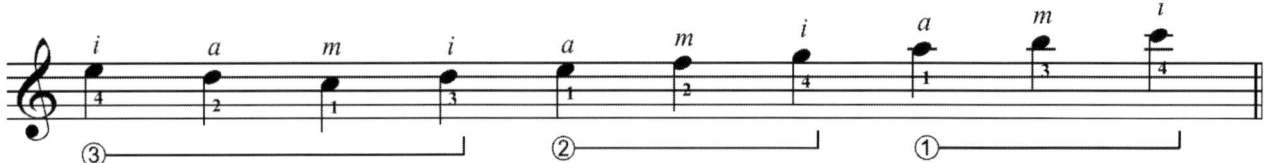

Figure 3.11: 4-note turnaround

Figure 3.12

Figure 3.12: 4-note turnaround in opposite direction

Try to apply the above fingering to the opening scale of Heitor Villa-Lobos' Etude #7.

The next option is a particular variation of the 5-note turnaround. Again, this is only to be used at the outset of a scale, where the change of direction happens immediately. This is an example of an A-M string crossing that, while modifying our fundamental approach to fingering scales and crossing strings, proves to be more efficient in some cases.

Figure 3.13

Figure 3.13: variation of the 5-note turnaround

Figure 3.14

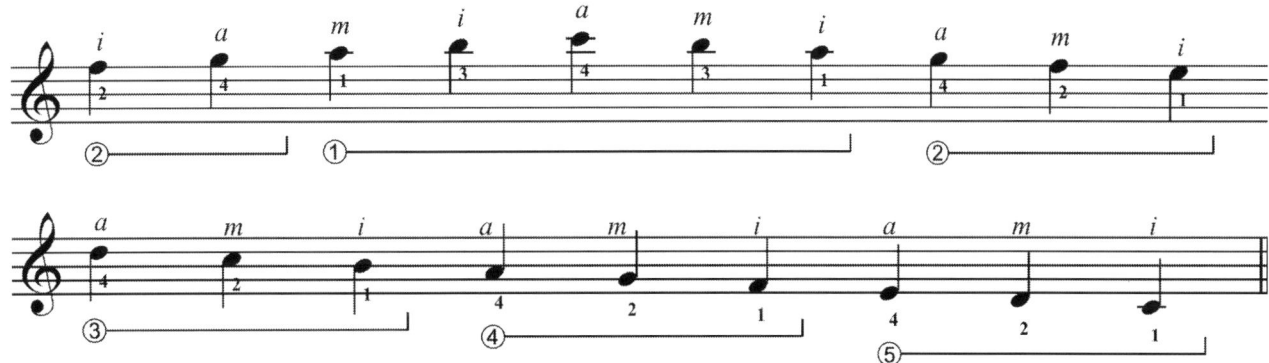

Figure 3.14: another variation of the 5-note turnaround

While the above figures bend some rules we have established, they are quite desirable in certain circumstances. I frequently use these fingerings to avoid the inevitable M-I-M-I alternation that often sets up a 5-note turnaround. Can you find a more efficient way to initiate the scale below?

Vicente Asencio, *La Joia* from *Collectici íntim*

© 1988 Schott Music GmbH & Co KG, Mainz – Germany. All rights reserved. Used by permission of European American Music Distributors LLC, sole U.S. and Canadian agent for Schott Music GmbH & Co KG, Mainz – Germany.

Alternate string crossings create the possibility of other turnarounds, the most useful of which is the 1-note turnaround (distinct from the turnaround using the thumb discussed previously). This technique is set up by placing two notes on the string just before the change of direction occurs. It can be used both ascending and descending, and keeps the A-M-I sequence unbroken. Keep in mind that this turnaround places us in a new position of the scale.

Figure 3.15

Figure 3.15: variation of the 1-note turnaround

Musical Application 2

Example 3-1. Vicente Asencio, *La Joia* from *Collectici íntim*

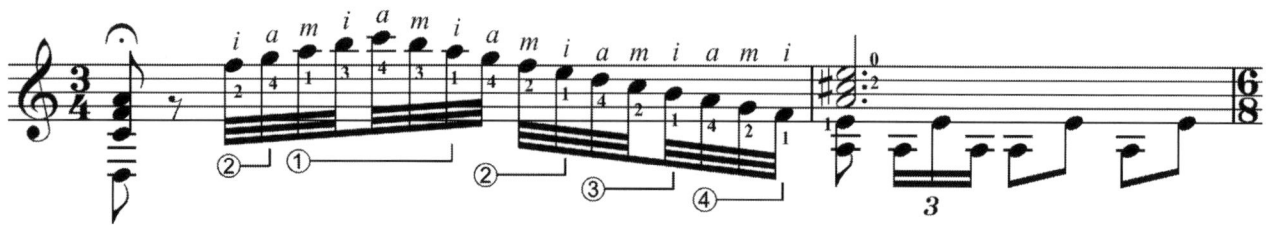

© 1988 Schott Music GmbH & Co KG, Mainz – Germany. All rights reserved. Used by permission of European American Music Distributors LLC, sole U.S. and Canadian agent for Schott Music GmbH & Co KG, Mainz – Germany.

Example 3-2. Matteo Carcassi, *Air Varie* Op. 8, Var. I

Example 3-3. Joaquín Rodrigo, *Un tiempo fue Itálica famosa*

Used with kind permission of European American Music Distributors LLC, sole U.S. and Canadian agent for Schott Music GmbH & Co KG, Mainz – Germany.

Chromatic Scales and Complex Figures

Playing chromatic scales and other complex figures with A-M-I technique can be tricky. Because the number of attacks per string varies significantly when arranging these scales, we end up with unusual string crossings in the right hand. In the majority of our previous exercises, we avoided alternate string crossings in favor of crossing with the A finger. With this problem, we have the opportunity to expand the possibilities of the technique without completely abandoning the principles we have established.

Below is a descending chromatic scale in open position. Note the string crossings with M and I throughout. Similar string crossings occur when playing ascending chromatic scales.

Figure 3.16

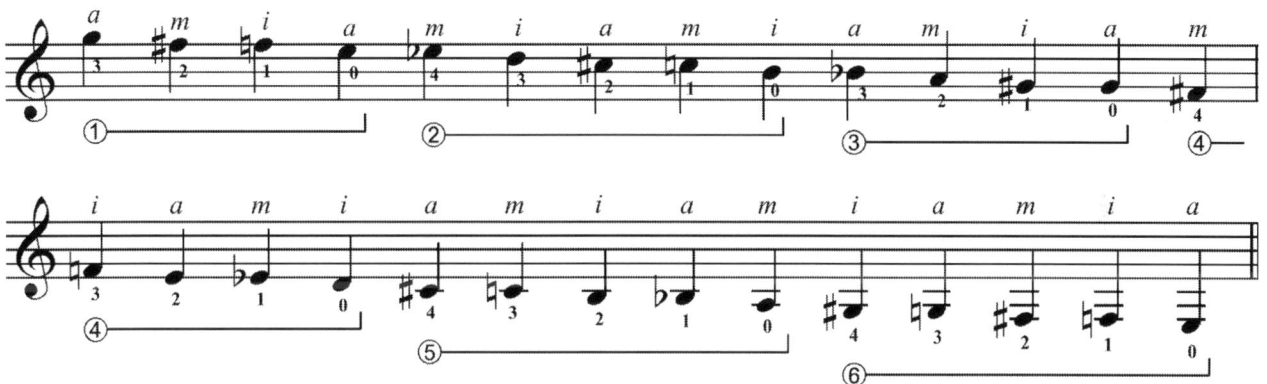

Figure 3.16: descending chromatic scale

Below are a few string crossing exercises to assist in developing the technique necessary to play chromatic scales and complex patterns with a continuous A-M-I sequence. The first is a simple six-note pattern that focuses upon the descending A-M string crossing.

Exercise 3.3

Exercise 3.3: string crossing exercise

The next exercise is the reverse of the above pattern, and helps to develop the ascending A-M string crossing.

Exercise 3.4

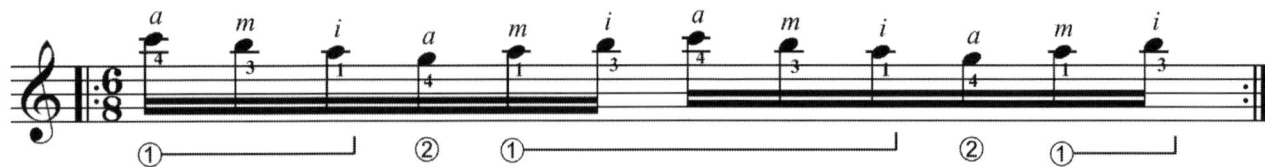

Exercise 3.4: string crossing exercise

Exercise 3.5 is a more complex pattern that helps to develop the descending A-M and M-I string crossings. Exercise 3.6 reverses the pattern, and assists in the development of the ascending A-M and M-I string crossings.

Exercise 3.5

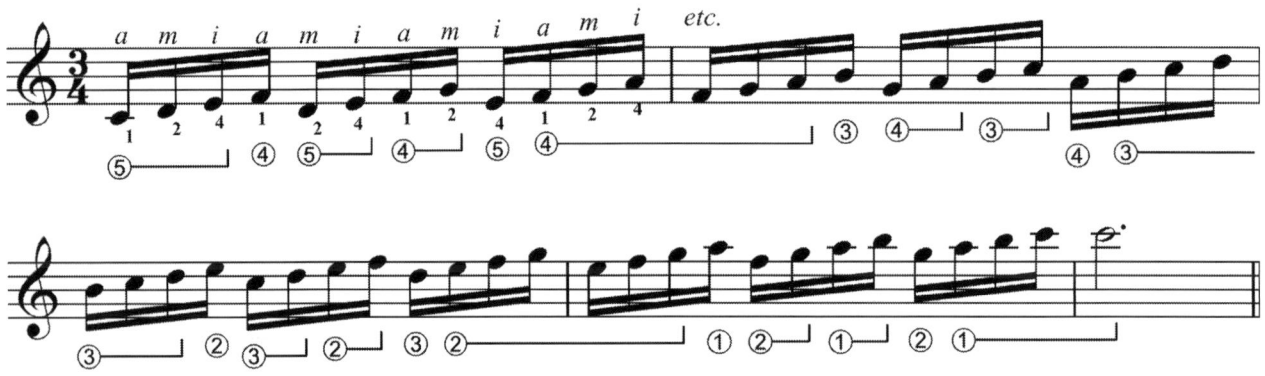

Exercise 3.5: string crossing exercise

Exercise 3.6

Exercise 3.6: string crossing exercise

Here are some other solutions for chromatic scales. The first makes use of the thumb and works great for ascending scales in higher positions of the guitar. If given the opportunity, I generally arrange the scale so the attack of P occurs on a strong beat.

Figure 3.17

Figure 3.17: chromatic scale using P

The next solution for chromatic scales is a three-note per string arrangement – Paul Gilbert style. This is quite unusual to see on the classical guitar, particularly with our larger scale instruments. However, I can play this pattern faster than any other chromatic scale pattern. It keeps a strict A-M-I sequence, and does not require any unusual string crossings with the right hand. There are multiple shifts involved, but it is very effective to use when playing fast chromatic scales. That said, I generally only use this pattern over short distances – three or four strings. Observe the use of left-hand finger 4 on the last note of the second and third strings. This fingering helps make the shifts easier.

Figure 3.18

Figure 3.18: three-note per string chromatic scale

Many complex patterns exist that may require modifications to this technique. A clever approach to left-hand fingerings will generally allow the use of the technique in these instances. Often I have found that the use of the thumb, slurs, and various turnaround formulas will allow me to continue or immediately return to the standard use of A-M-I technique. At times, though, it may be impossible to use the technique in the ways outlined in previous sections. The possibilities for solutions may be endless – certainly far too numerous to list within the scope of this method. However, I have included my fingerings to a few passages from the standard repertoire to serve as examples for alternative uses of the technique.

Musical Application 3

Example 3-4. Francisco Tárrega, *Capricho Arabe*

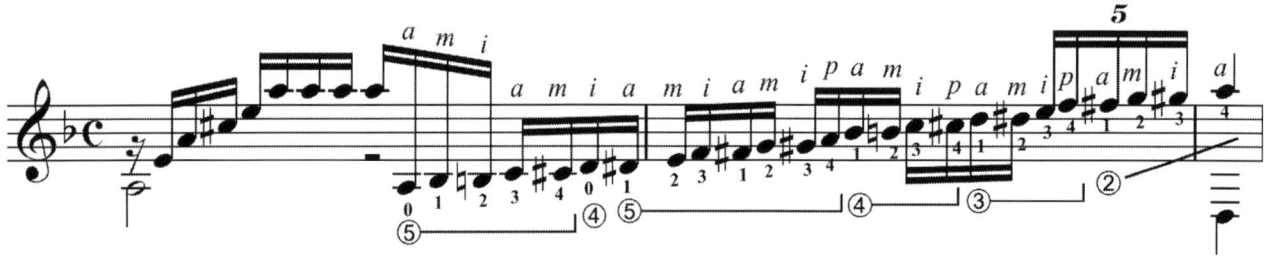

Example 3-5. Luigi Legnani, Caprice 36

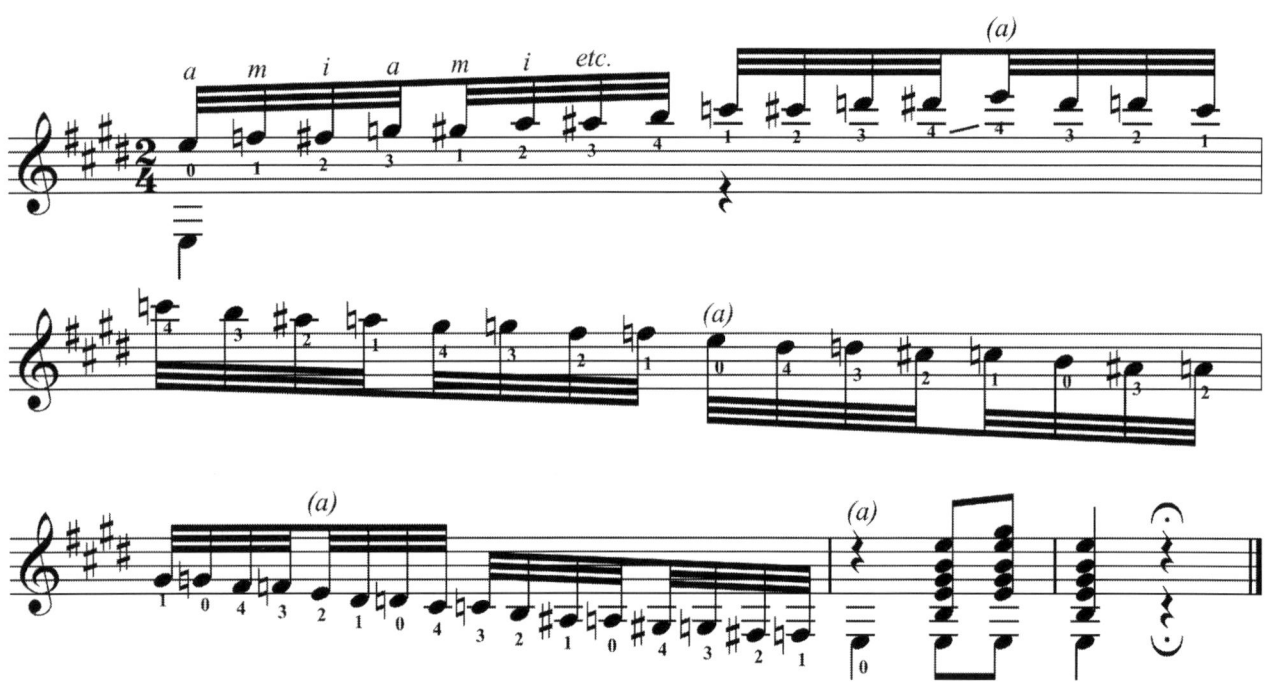

Example 3-6. Joaquín Turina, *Sonata para guitarra* Op. 61, I. *Allegro*

© 1932 Schott Music GmbH & Co KG, Mainz – Germany. © renewed. All rights reserved. Used by permission of European American Music Distributors LLC, sole U.S. and Canadian agent for Schott Music GmbH & Co KG, Mainz – Germany.

Example 3-7. Joaquín Rodrigo, *Un tiempo fue Itálica famosa*

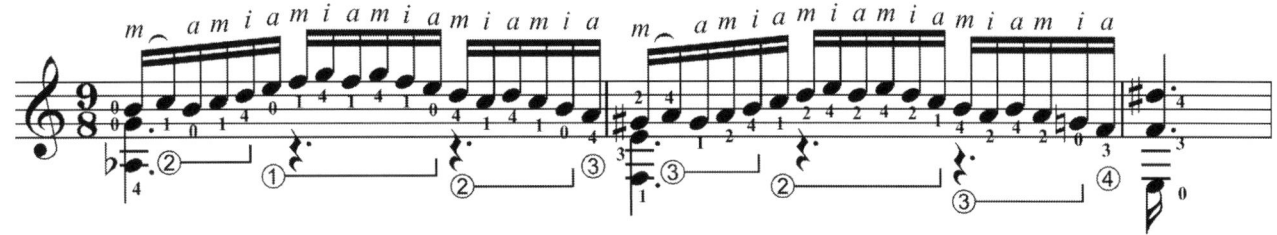

Used with kind permission of European American Music Distributors LLC, sole U.S. and Canadian agent for Schott Music GmbH & Co KG, Mainz – Germany.

Example 3-8. Agustín Barrios, *Vals* Op.8, No. 4

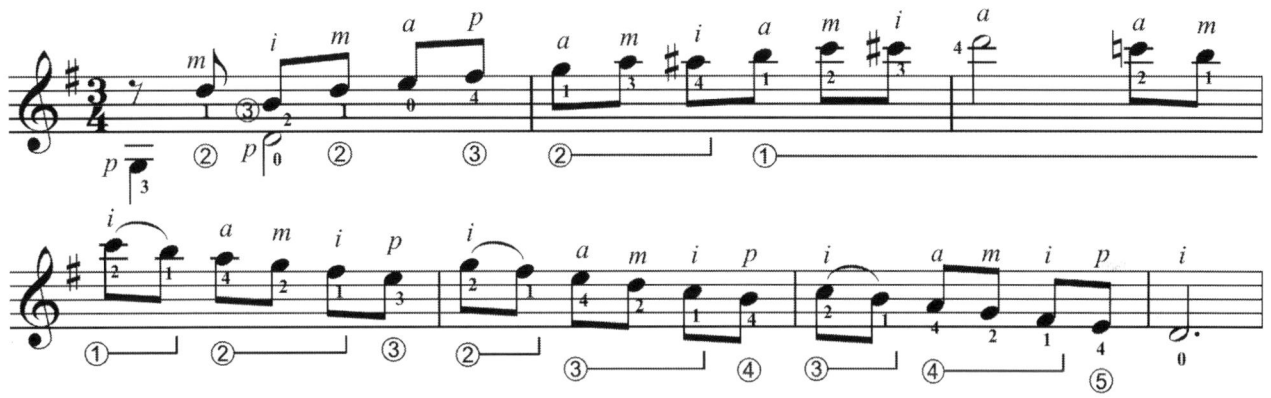

Example 3-9. Repeated notes figure (four attacks per string)

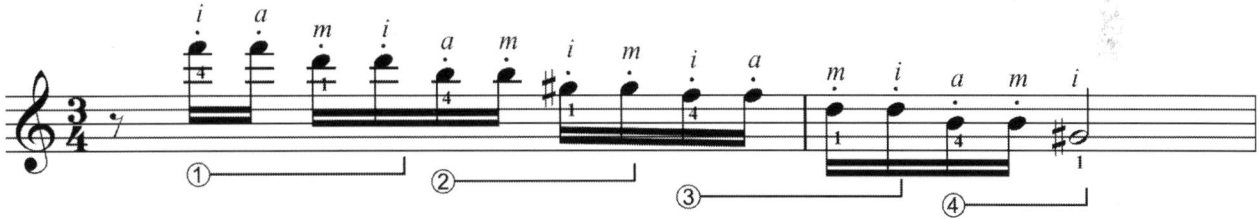

The example above shows a solution to a series of repeated notes that outlines a chord. Figures such as this are fairly common in the guitar repertoire. Try the same right-hand fingering in Mario Castelnuovo-Tedesco's *Capriccio Diabolico* Op. 85, at the section marked *Con Fuoco*. Arrange the passage so there are four attacks per string.

The Ascending Shift

When the musical context demands that we shift from one position to another, we are faced with several problems with the consistency of our technique. As I have stated, we want to maintain the motion towards the thumb as much as possible, preferably A-M-I. We will first address the ascending shift out of the open position.

The most advantageous time to shift out of the open position coincides with the attack of an open string. This brief amount of time allows us to reposition the left hand and continue the passage in the next position. In a piece of music, I generally prefer to shift as early as possible within the course of a scale. Doing so allows for greater possibilities of creating musical gestures safely. Much harm can be done to the musical intent when an accelerando or crescendo is accompanied by a difficult shift near its climax.

The figures below show several options of completing the same scale by utilizing different methods of shifting. I wrote the same scale for each option so that the differences and advantages of each would be clear. These examples simply complete two octaves of a certain scale. Of course, you may continue playing notes beyond those written here, and play the same patterns beginning on different strings or in different keys. Within a piece of music, the method of shifting you choose to employ will obviously be determined by the context of the music. If you can choose *any* option below, choose the one that works best for you. The figures below all ascend from the open 6th string. If you are starting from another note, consult the previous section on beginning the ascending scale for alternative options.

Shifting to Positions V & VI

Figure 3.19 is an excellent option to keep the A-M-I motion consistent. This type of shift contains the string crossing A-M on strings 5 and 6, respectively, and continues with the index finger. By using this fingering, a consistent A-M-I motion is maintained. Observe how the right-hand fingering after the shift is the same as Figure 2.6 in the section on beginning the ascending scale.

Figure 3.19

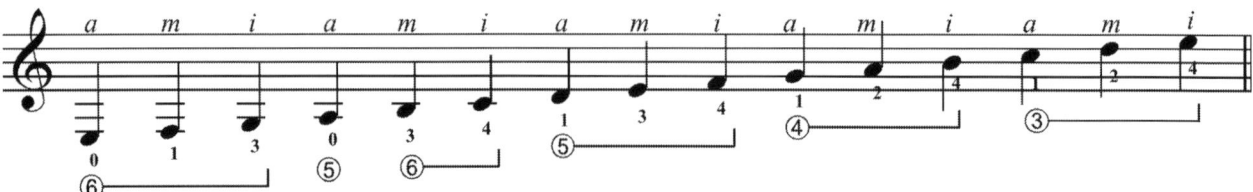

Figure 3.19: shifting on the open 5th string to position V

Figures 3.20 and 3.21 contain a similar shifting technique as found in Figure 3.19. However, these figures demonstrate the shift on alternate scale degrees.

Figure 3.20

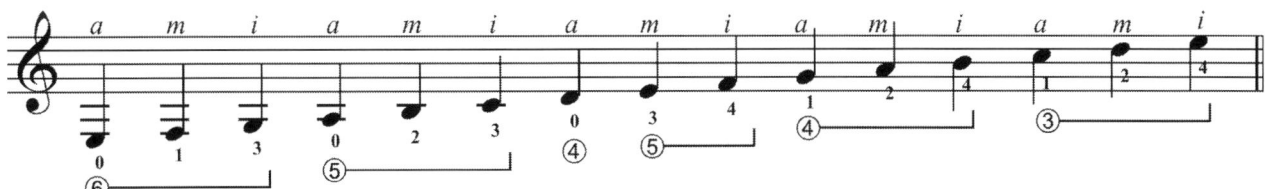

Figure 3.20: shifting on the open 4th string to position V

Figure 3.21

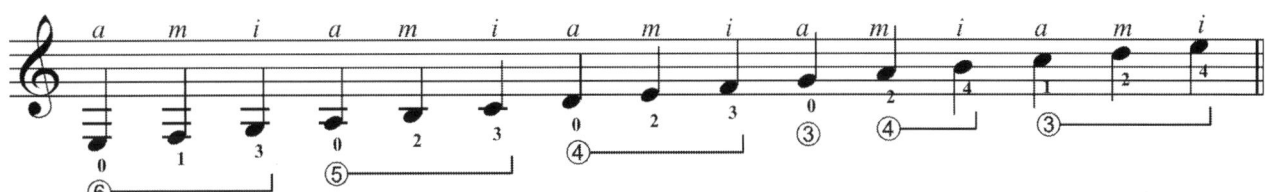

Figure 3.21: shifting on the open 3rd string to position V

It is also possible to use a slur immediately after the shift. In such a case, the right-hand attack of choice would be P, as this technique is often used to initiate an ascending scale (see Figure 2.7) and does not change the direction of motion of the right hand towards the thumb. The following figures are identical to the figures above with the addition of a post-shift slur.

Figure 3.22

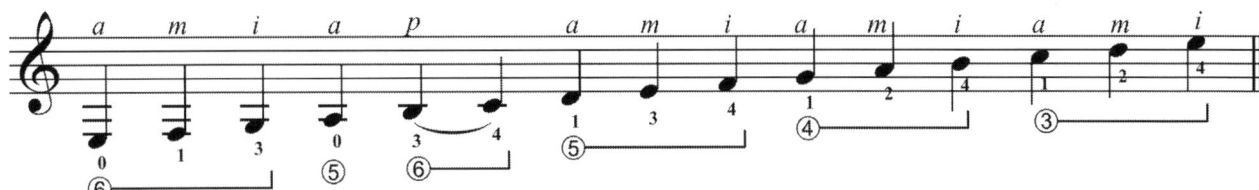

Figure 3.22: use of a 3-4 slur on the 6th string following the shift

Figure 3.23

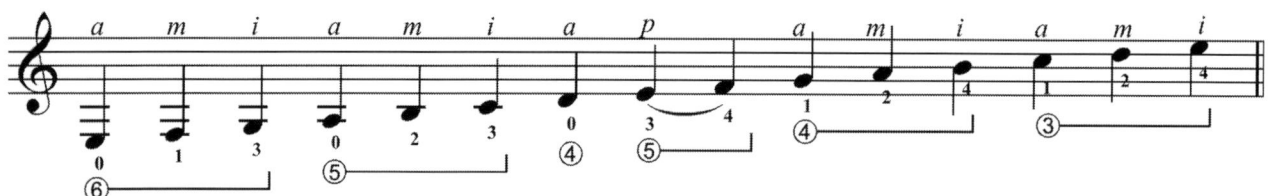

Figure 3.23: use of a 3-4 slur on the 5th string following the shift

Figure 3.24

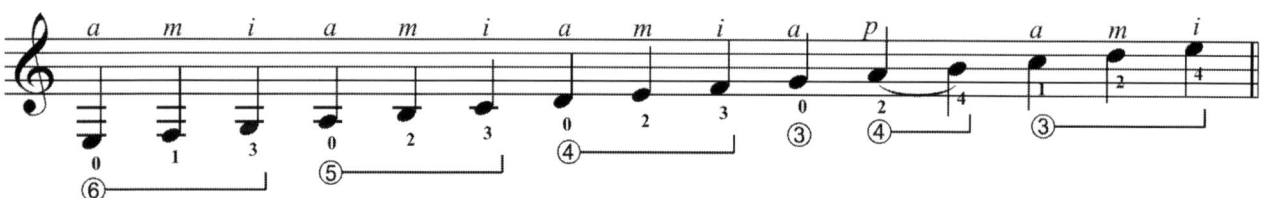

Figure 3.24: use of a 2-4 slur on the 4th string following the shift

Shifting to Positions III & IV

Now that I have discussed the use of P following a shift, I feel I can properly introduce the shifts to positions III and IV. In these shifts, the only way to meet our goal of motion towards the thumb is to use P immediately after the shift. I believe you will find this to be a comfortable sequence of fingering. The right-hand fingering following the shift is identical to the fingering from Figure 2.9 in the section on beginning the ascending scale.

Figure 3.25

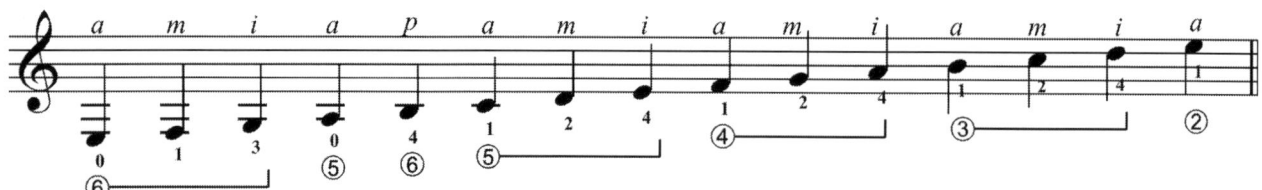

Figure 3.25: shifting on the open 5th string to position III

Figure 3.26

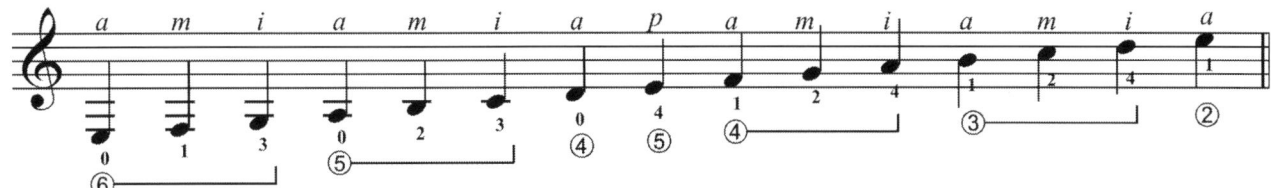

Figure 3.26: shifting on the open 4th string to position III

The following is an example of a shift into position IV. There is virtually no difference in the action required to execute such a shift.

Figure 3.27

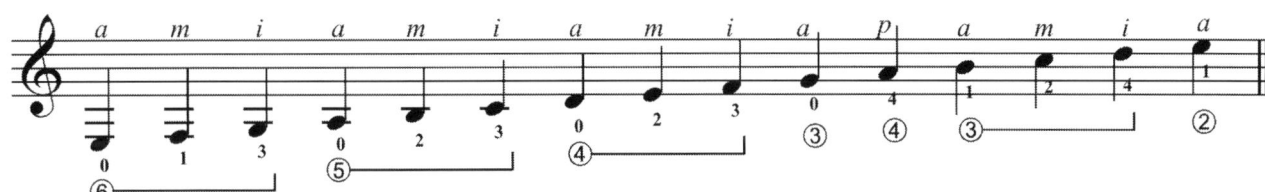

Figure 3.27: shifting on the open 3rd string to position IV

Note that in most common keys this type of shift will normally put us in position IV, as in Figure 3.27 and the following example. The exceptions are most of C major, F major, and some of the shifts in their relative minor keys.

Figure 3.28

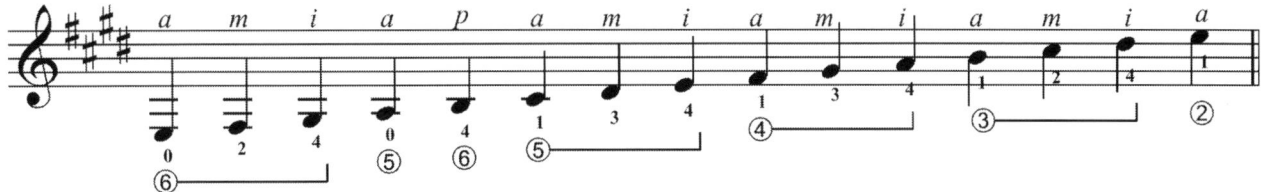

Figure 3.28: shifting on the open 5th string to position IV in E major

Shifting to Position VII

Shifting to this position can be somewhat problematic. In the figures above, we used the A finger on the open string just before the shift, followed by attacks of M-I or P in the new position. When shifting to position VII, we have three notes on the initial string after the shift. We have in effect run out of right-hand fingers needed to complete the scale in the fashions listed above. However, the use of P or some well-placed slurs can generally alleviate most of these problems. We also have the option of beginning the scale with I. Doing so allows us to continue a steady A-M-I pattern when we reach position VII. The examples below are a few of my solutions to shift effectively to position VII.

Figure 3.29

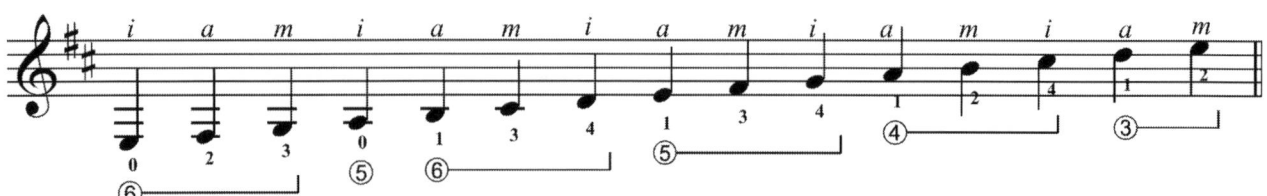

Figure 3.29: shifting to position VII beginning with the I finger

Figure 3.30

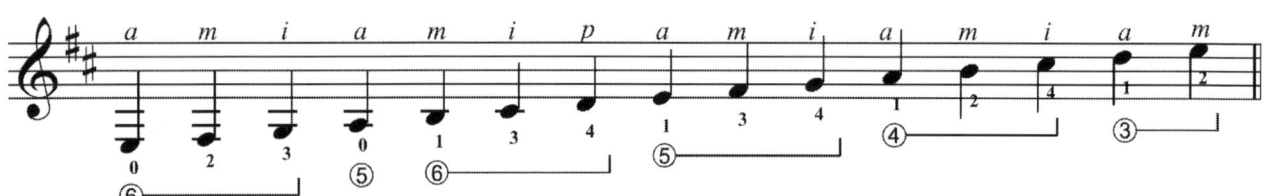

Figure 3.30: shifting to position VII with uninterrupted articulation (beginning with A finger)

Figure 3.31

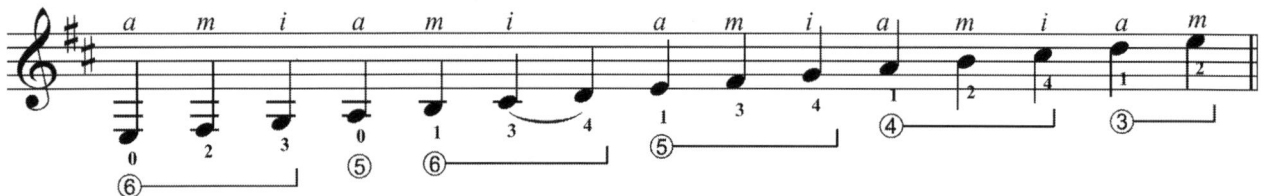

Figure 3.31: shifting to position VII using a 3-4 slur

Figure 3.32

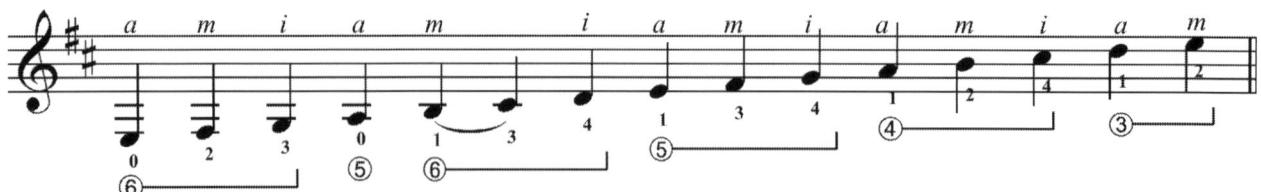

Figure 3.32: shifting to position VII using a 1-3 slur over a continuous A-M-I pattern

Figure 3.33

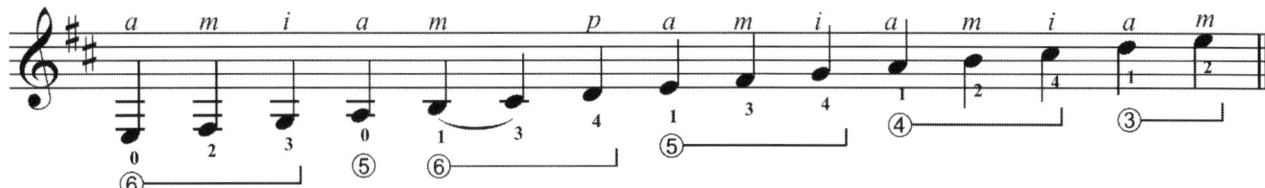

Figure 3.33: shifting to position VII using a 1-3 slur followed by an attack of P

The following figures contain multiple slurs over a single attack of the right hand. Such techniques are scarcely used in traditional approaches to classical guitar technique. However, I have used the following solutions to a very satisfying end in passages where a legato effect is desirable. Slurs with three or more notes generally sound best in the bass range of the guitar, where the sound is still strong. Figure 3.35 is particularly effective for initiating a legato scale with a crescendo.

Figure 3.34

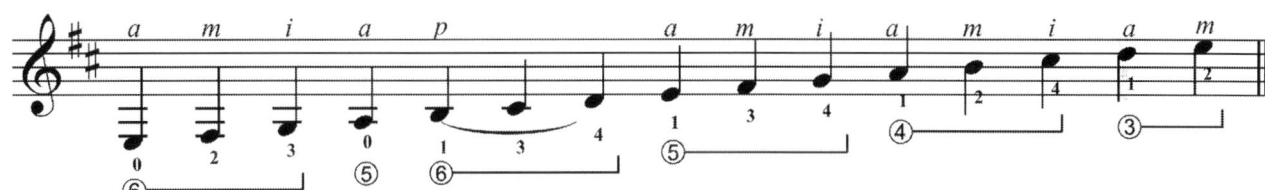

Figure 3.34: shifting to position VII using a 3-note slur

Figure 3.35

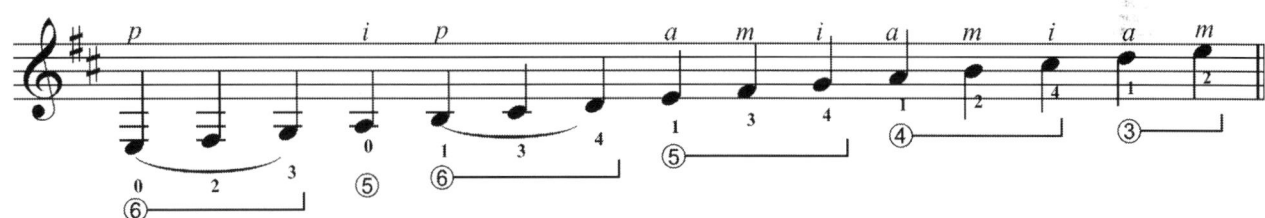

Figure 3.35: shifting to position VII using multiple 3-note slurs (great for crescendos)

Shifting to Positions VIII & IX

The method used to shift to positions VIII and IX is similar to the method of shifting to positions III and IV. The obvious difference here is the necessity to play in the open position *at least* (determined by key) until we reach the open 4th string. By doing so, we are given our first chance to play the 12th fret E of the 6th string. Again, following the shift the right-hand finger of choice would be the thumb, followed by

A-M-I. Continuing these scales upward would land us beyond the 12th fret of the 1st string, making these shifts effective tools for reaching the higher registers of the guitar.

Figure 3.36

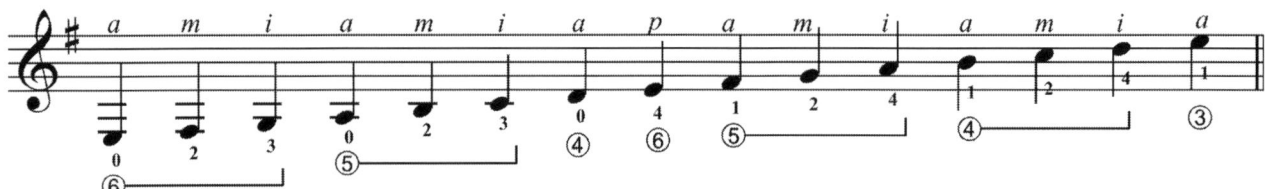

Figure 3.36: shifting on the open 4th string to position IX

Figure 3.37

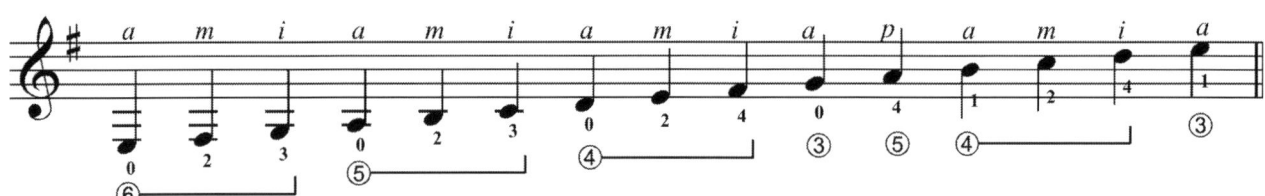

Figure 3.37: shifting on the open 3rd string to position IX

Shifting to Positions X & XI

Shifting to these positions is similar to shifting to positions V and VI. It may be more comfortable to attack with the right-hand thumb immediately after the shift, and to use the slur as in Figure 3.39.

Figure 3.38

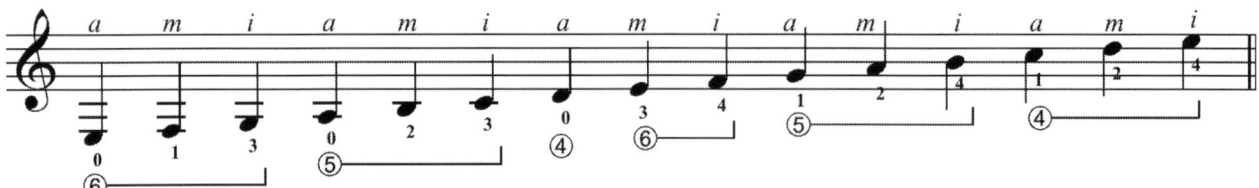

Figure 3.38: shifting to position X with an uninterrupted A-M-I

Figure 3.39

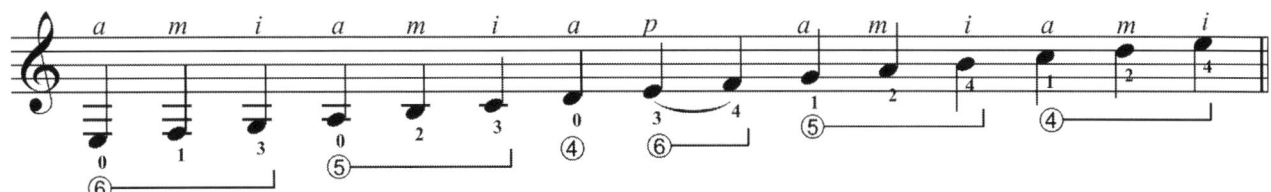

Figure 3.39: shifting to position X with the use of P and a 3-4 slur

Shifting to Position XII

Now we are getting up there! And, to be quite honest, we are approaching the limit of our present shifting technique. Though the guitar is somewhat difficult to tune in this area, I have found use for these shifts – rarely. There are other solutions for reaching the highest registers of our instrument (which will be discussed shortly), but for the sake of exhausting all of our present possibilities I will continue with these exercises. There are other right-hand solutions for the following figures, which can be found above in the section on shifting to position VII (they share the same possibilities).

Figure 3.40

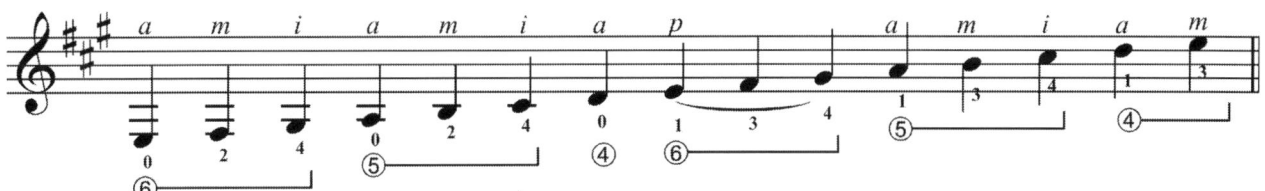

Figure 3.40: shifting to position XII with 3-note slur

Figure 3.41

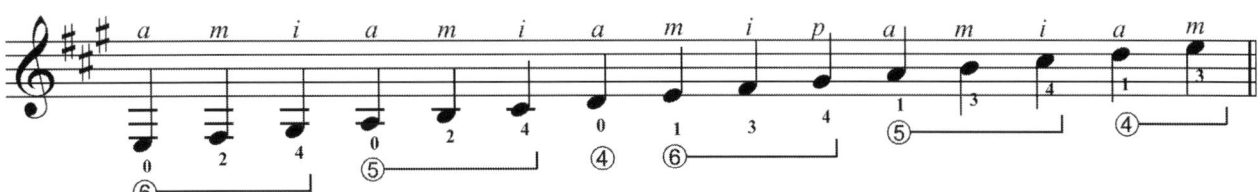

Figure 3.41: shifting to position XII with uninterrupted articulation

The Descending Shift

The descending shift shares many of the same basic principles as the ascending shift discussed above. One major difference is that, when descending, the attack of P always comes before the shift occurs. This technique allows for a very comfortable sequence of attacks with the right hand, as we are playing directly to the thumb – like the fingering of an A-M-I-P arpeggio.

Figure 3.42

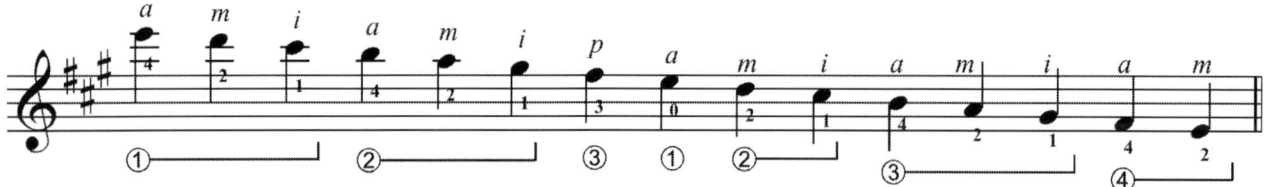

Figure 3.42: descending shift using P pre-shift

Figure 3.43

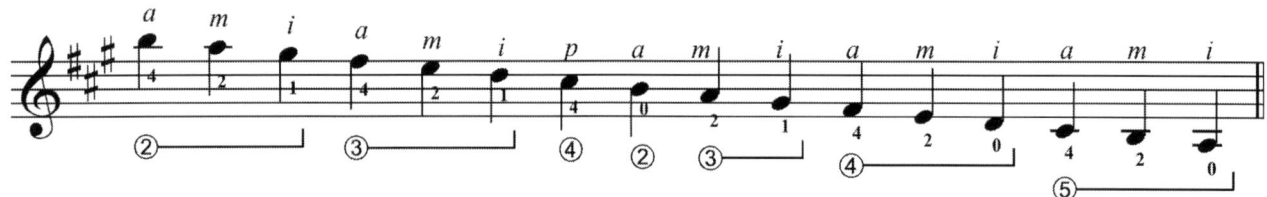

Figure 3.43: descending shift on an alternate scale degree

The above figures contain one note on the final string before the shift occurs. It is also possible to use two and three notes on this final string pre-shift. The following figures show these possibilities, and present alternate fingering options for each instance. Here are the two-note solutions.

Figure 3.44

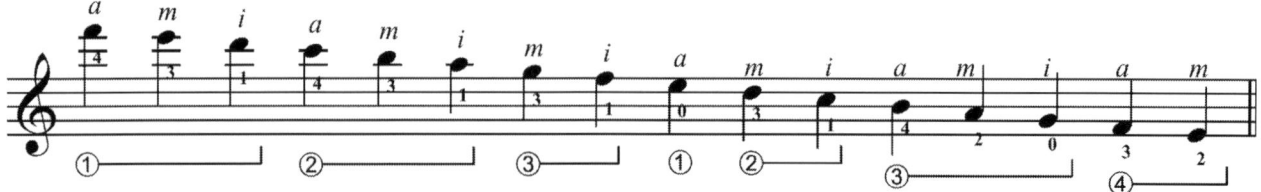

Figure 3.44: descending scale with uninterrupted articulation

Figure 3.45

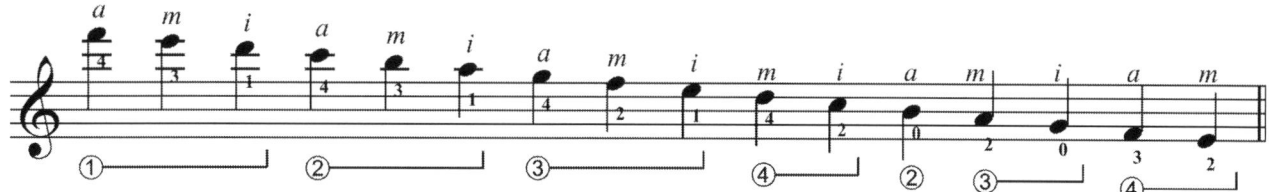

Figure 3.45: same technique as Figure 3.44 with shift on an alternate scale degree

Figure 3.46

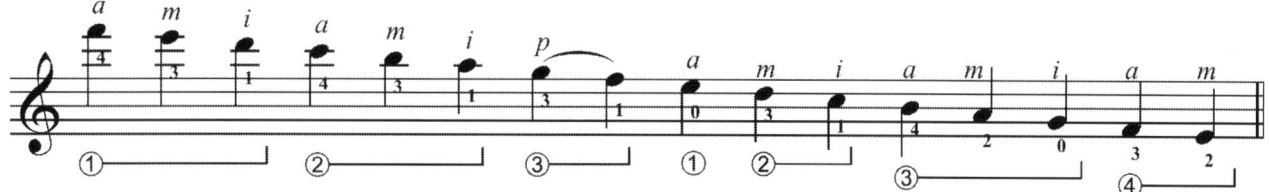

Figure 3.46: descending scale using P and a pre-shift slur

Figure 3.47

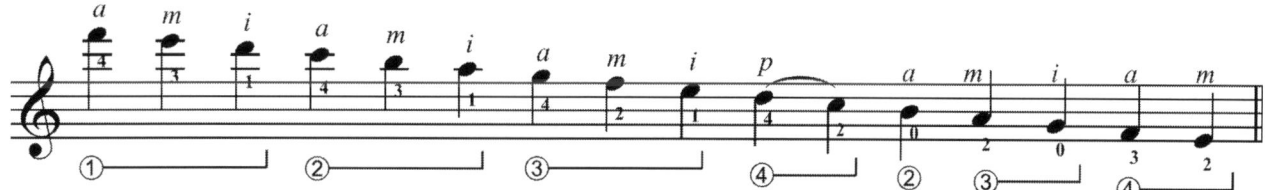

Figure 3.47: same technique as Figure 3.46 with shift on an alternate scale degree

At last, we reach the three-note pre-shift solutions. Unlike in ascending scales, I generally avoid slurring more than two notes when descending – particularly on the treble strings.

Figure 3.48

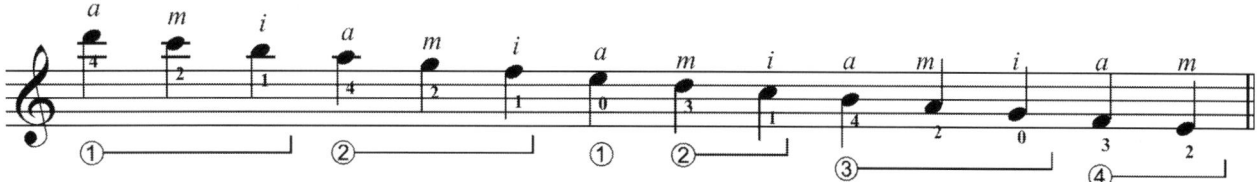

Figure 3.48: descending shift with three articulated notes on final string pre-shift

Figure 3.49

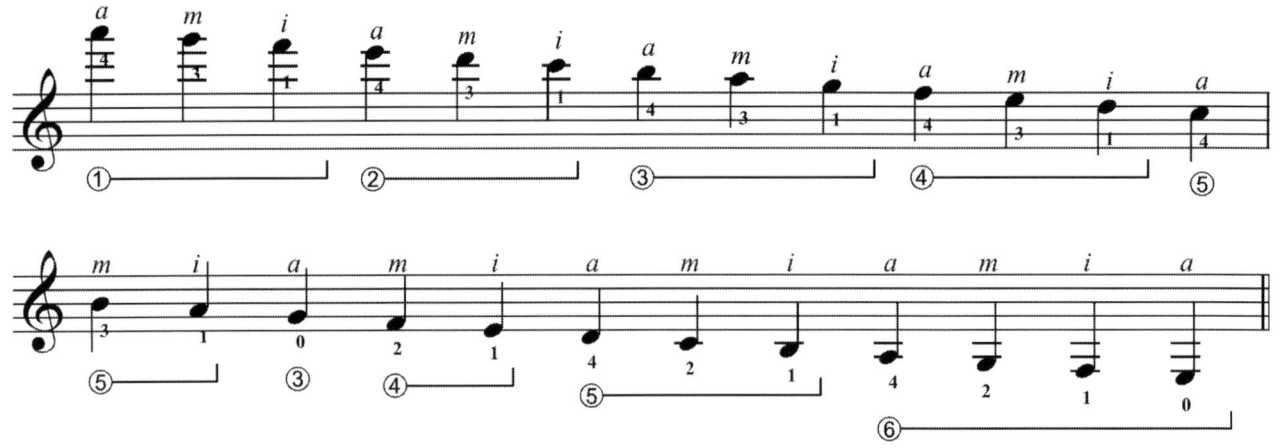

Figure 3.49: descending shift with three articulated notes on final string pre-shift

Figure 3.50

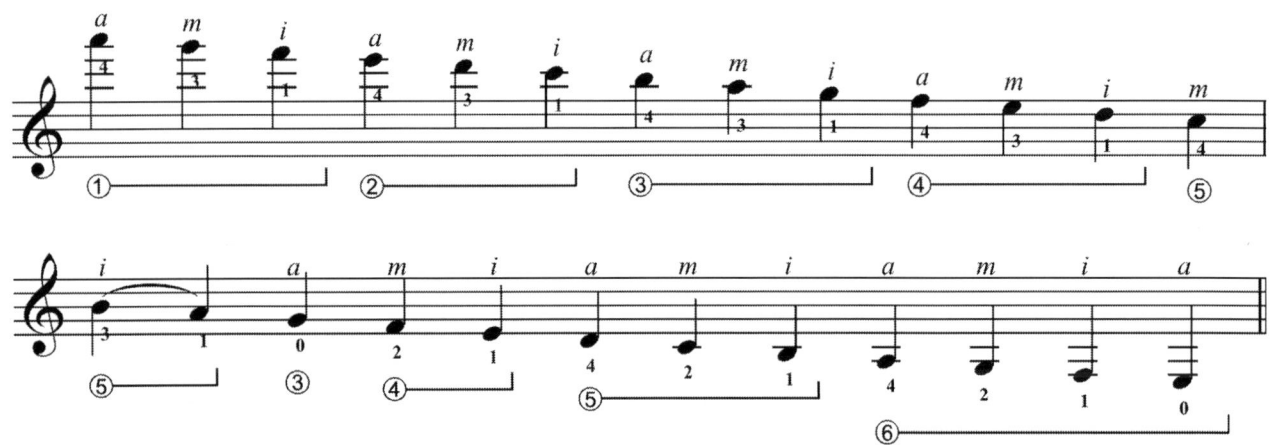

Figure 3.50: same as Figure 3.49 with a 2-note slur pre-shift

Notice in the above figures that following the shift we are in position II. Like in the previous figures, if the key signature allows we may shift at other scale degrees as well.

Shifting on a Single String

Of course, it is also possible to change positions without using an open string. In this technique, the most advantageous type of shift is a single-string repetition of A-M-I, resulting in six total attacks on the string.

Figure 3.51

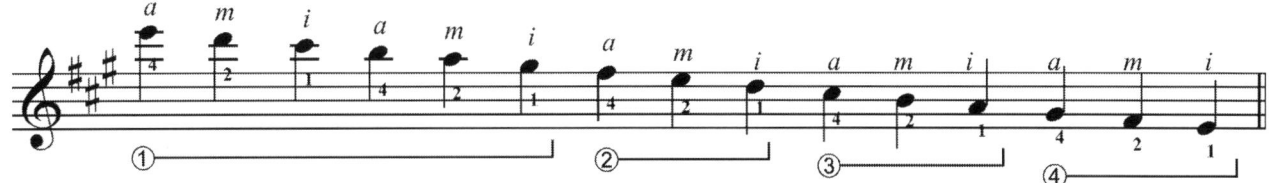

Figure 3.51: descending shift on a single string

Figure 3.52

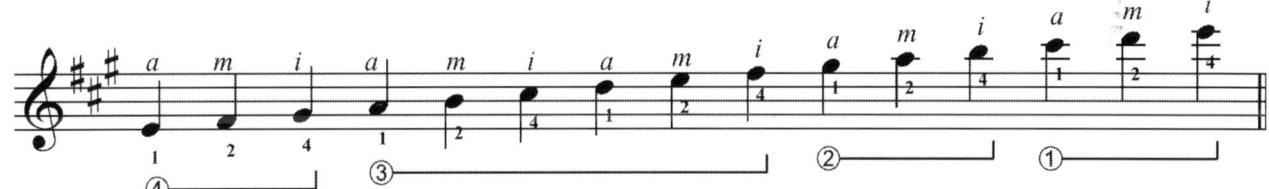

Figure 3.52: ascending shift on a single string

Note the continuous A-M-I right-hand fingering in the figures above. The left-hand technique required to execute such passages needs to be addressed here. When descending, finger 4 needs to begin the shifting motion as you are playing finger 1 pre-shift. When ascending, finger 1 should begin moving towards finger 4 as finger 4 is articulated. This pre-shift preparation will help to make this difficult transition smooth and effortless.

Exercise 3.7

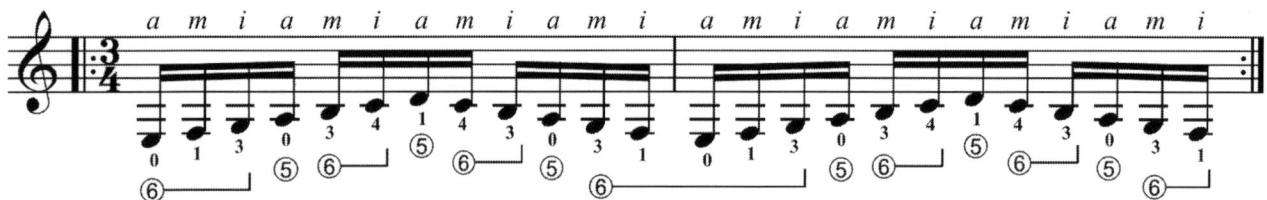

Exercise 3.7: shifting

Exercise 3.8

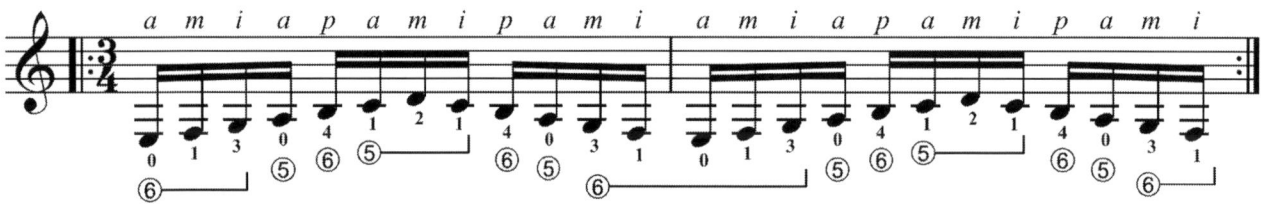

Exercise 3.8: shifting

Exercise 3.9

Exercise 3.9: shifting

Exercise 3.10

Exercise 3.10: exercise for R.H. string crossing sequence

Exercise 3.11

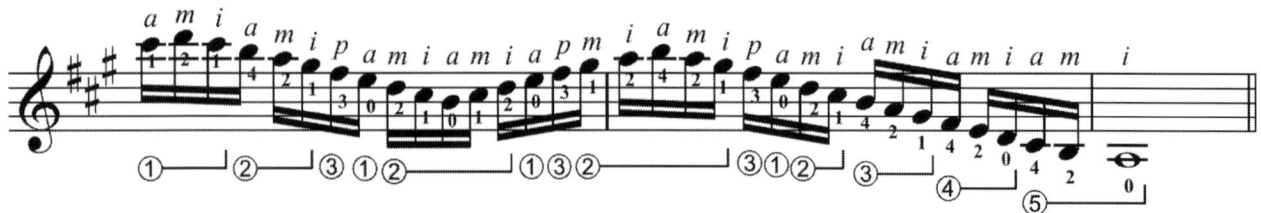

Exercise 3.11: shifting

Musical Application 4

Example 3-10. Dionisio Aguado, Rondo Op. 2, No. 2

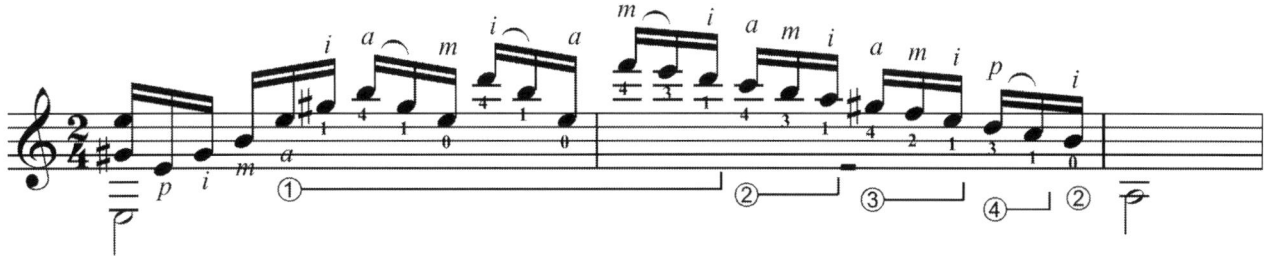

Example 3-11. Dionisio Aguado, Rondo Op. 2, No. 2 (alternate fingering)

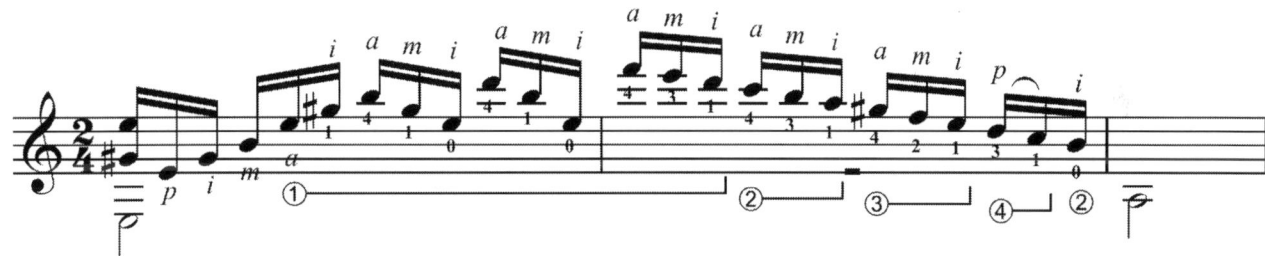

Example 3-12. Joaquín Rodrigo, *Concierto de Aranjuez*, III. *Allegro gentile*

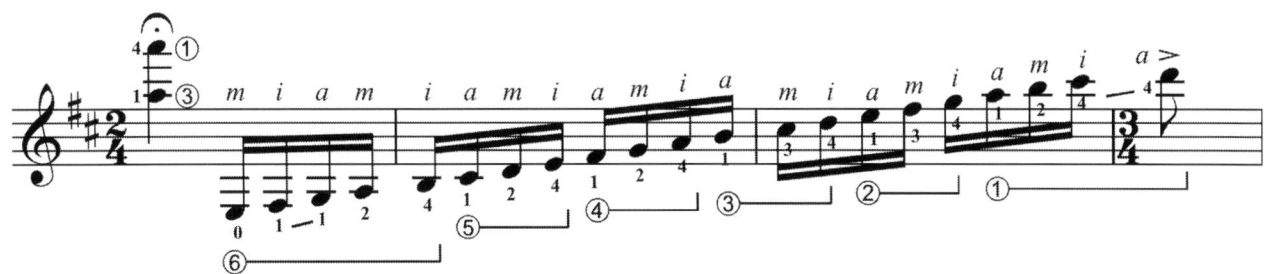

© 1959 Schott Music GmbH & Co KG, Mainz – Germany. © renewed. All rights reserved. Used in the World excluding Spain by permission of European American Music Distributors LLC, sole U.S. and Canadian agent for Schott Music GmbH & Co KG, Mainz – Germany.

Example 3-13. Mauro Giuliani, *Rossiniana* Op. 119

Example 3-14. Francisco Tárrega, *Estudio Brilliante*

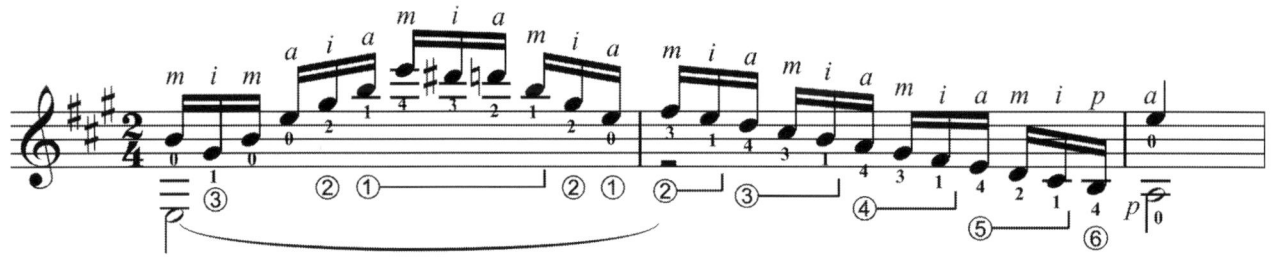

Example 3-15. Miguel Llobet, *Scherzo-Vals*

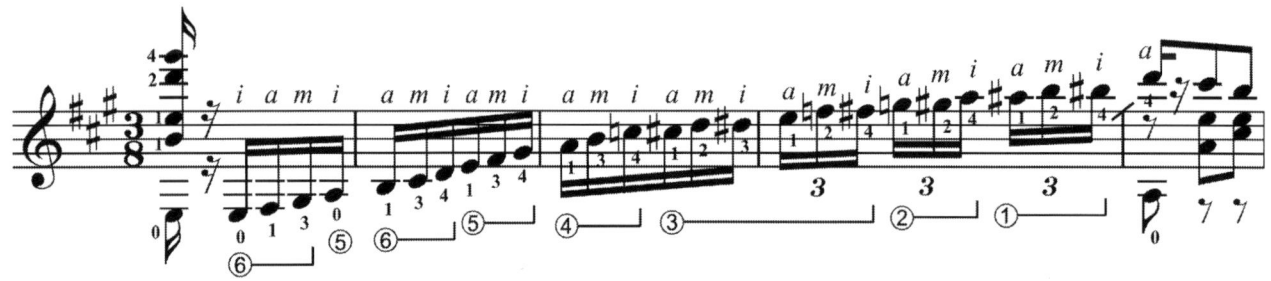

Example 3-16. Niccolò Paganini, *Grande Sonata in La Maggiore*, III. *Andantino Variato*

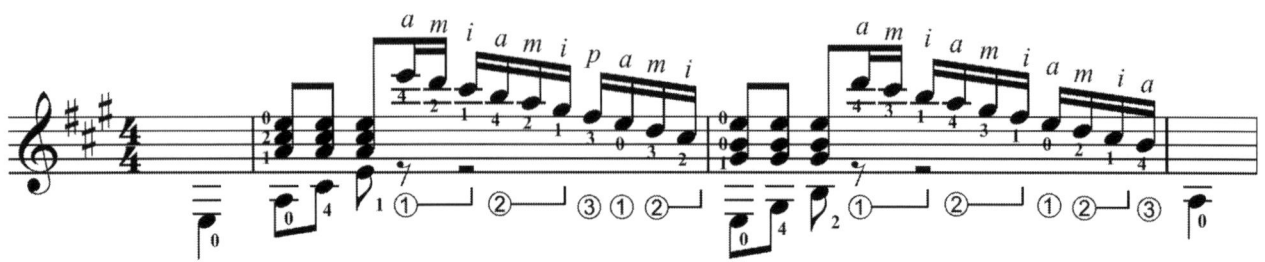

Closing Remarks

The content of this method provides the fundamentals to develop a solid A-M-I scale technique. As a point of departure and a framework to my process of fingering fast passages, this technique has become an integral aspect of my playing, and key to my development as a guitarist. It is my sincere hope that this method has proven helpful to you. With diligent study and eventual mastery, these techniques may assist you in the performance of virtuosic guitar repertoire. Above all, give these concepts and fingerings time to develop. As with any new technique, much time and deliberate practice is needed to enjoy success.

Scales Reference

Scales Reference

The final section of this method includes common scales arranged three notes per string. Each scale completes two octaves of a mode, and then continues on the 1st string to finish the notes in that position. When performing these scales as written, a 5-note turnaround must be executed on the 1st string to keep the A-M-I pattern consistent. Feel free to experiment with the techniques you have learned in this book. Try various turnarounds, shifts and patterns to add interest to your scale practice. For instance, a 6-note turnaround will allow you to effectively move to the next mode or position of the scale. Shifting on a single string will also accomplish this. Use the many types of open string shifts you have learned to reach or depart from the highest registers of the guitar. Try creating extended scales by using a combination of the above techniques. Finally, memorizing the shapes of these scales will allow you to quickly use them in any key.

C Major Positions

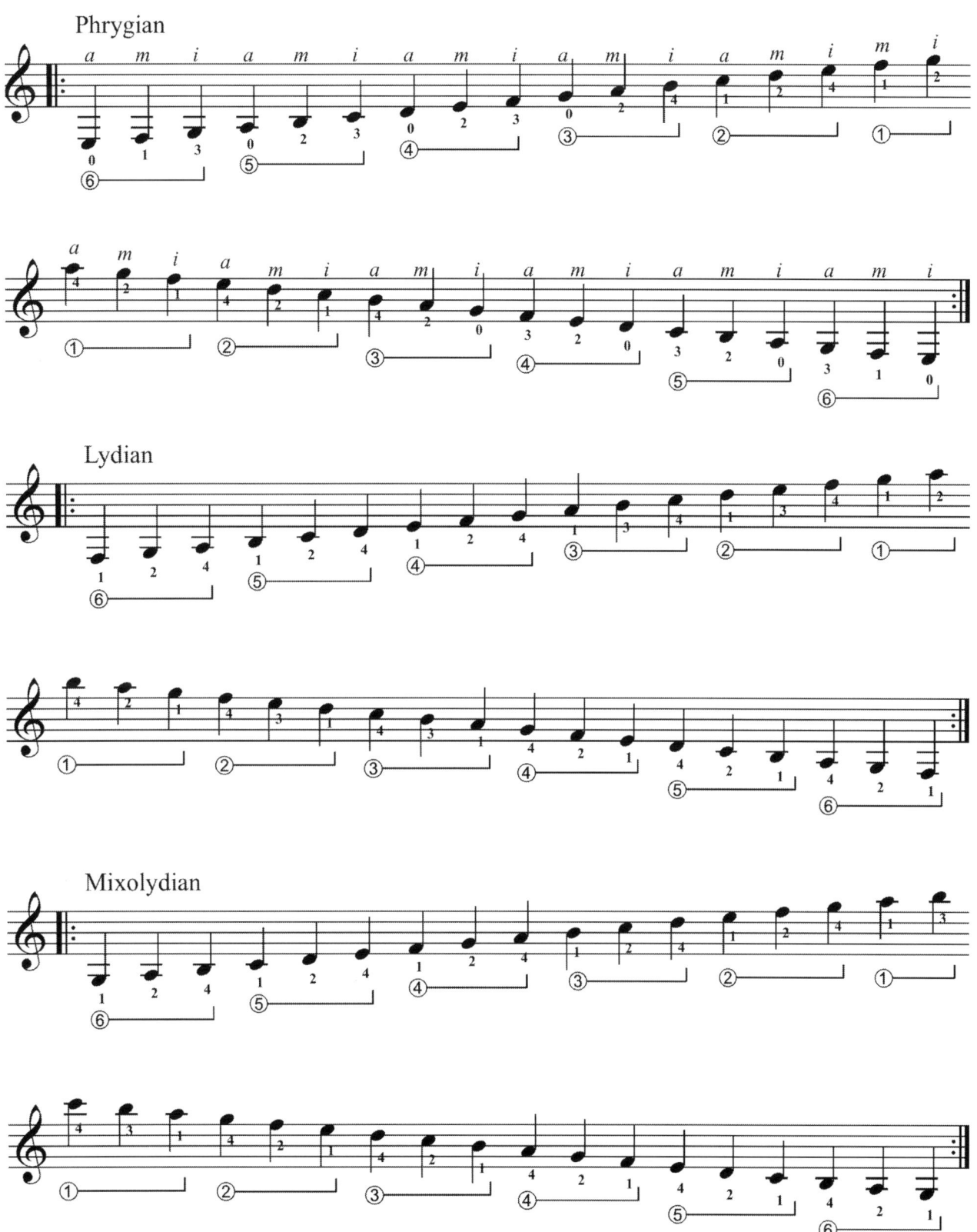

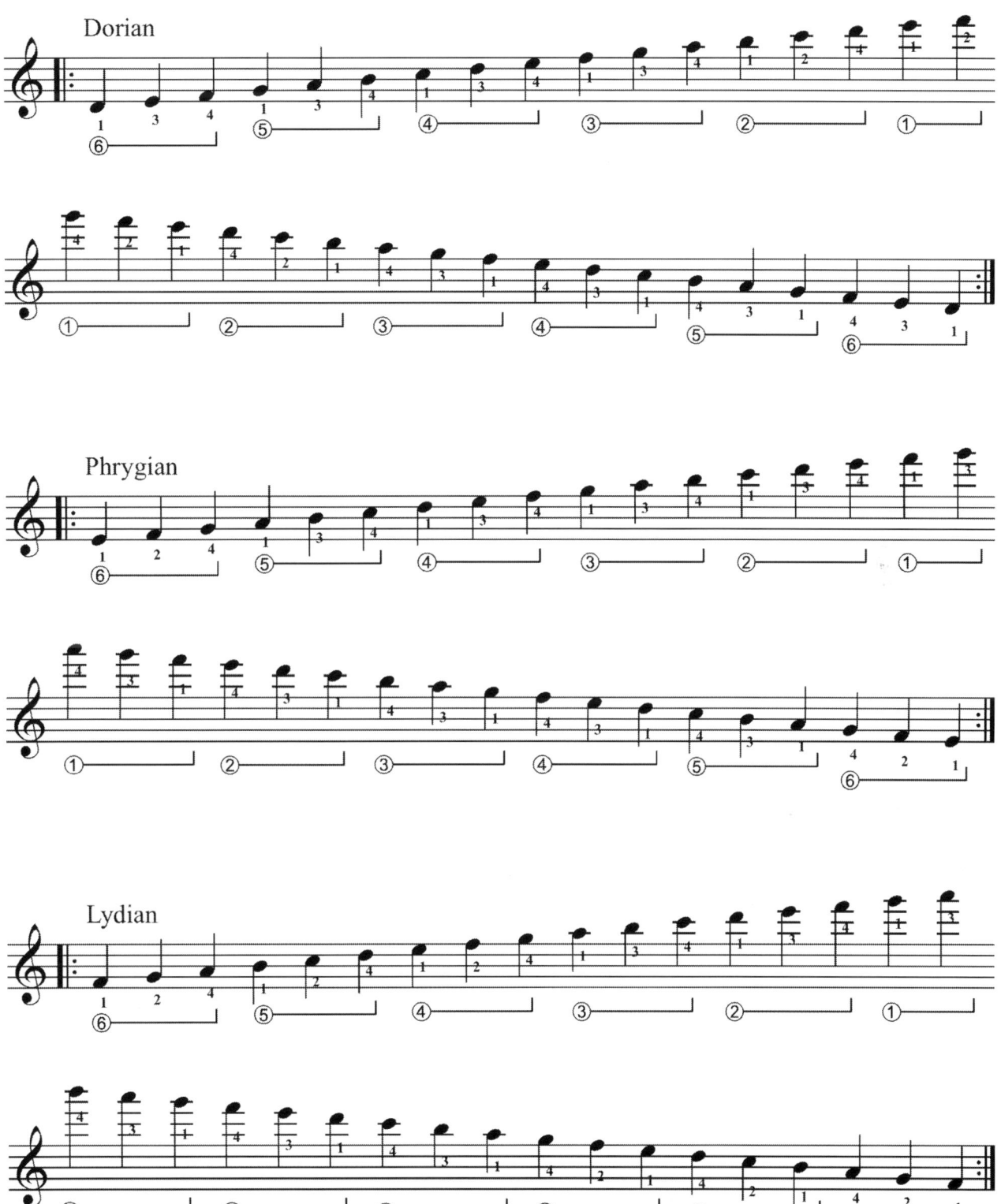

G Major Positions

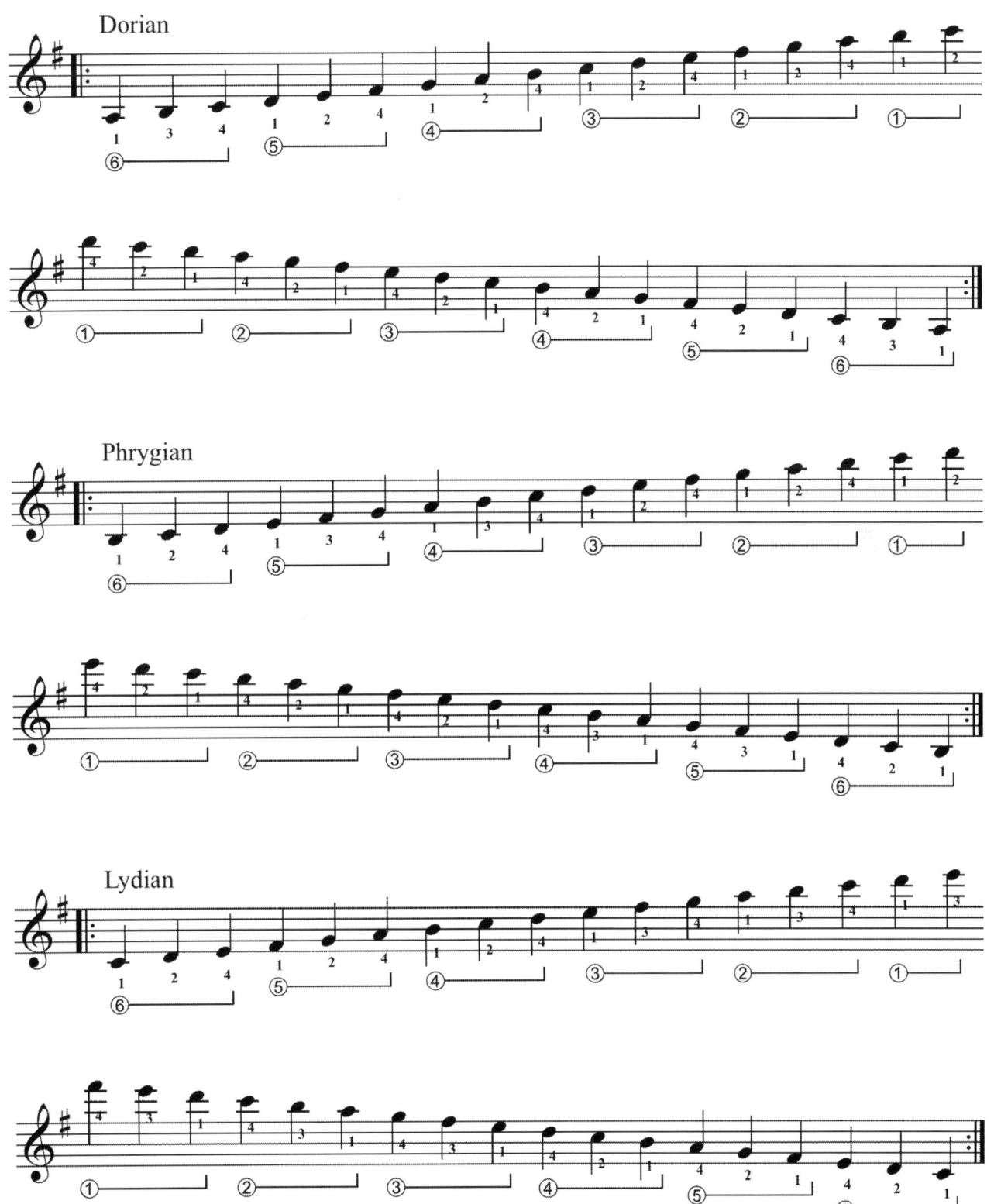

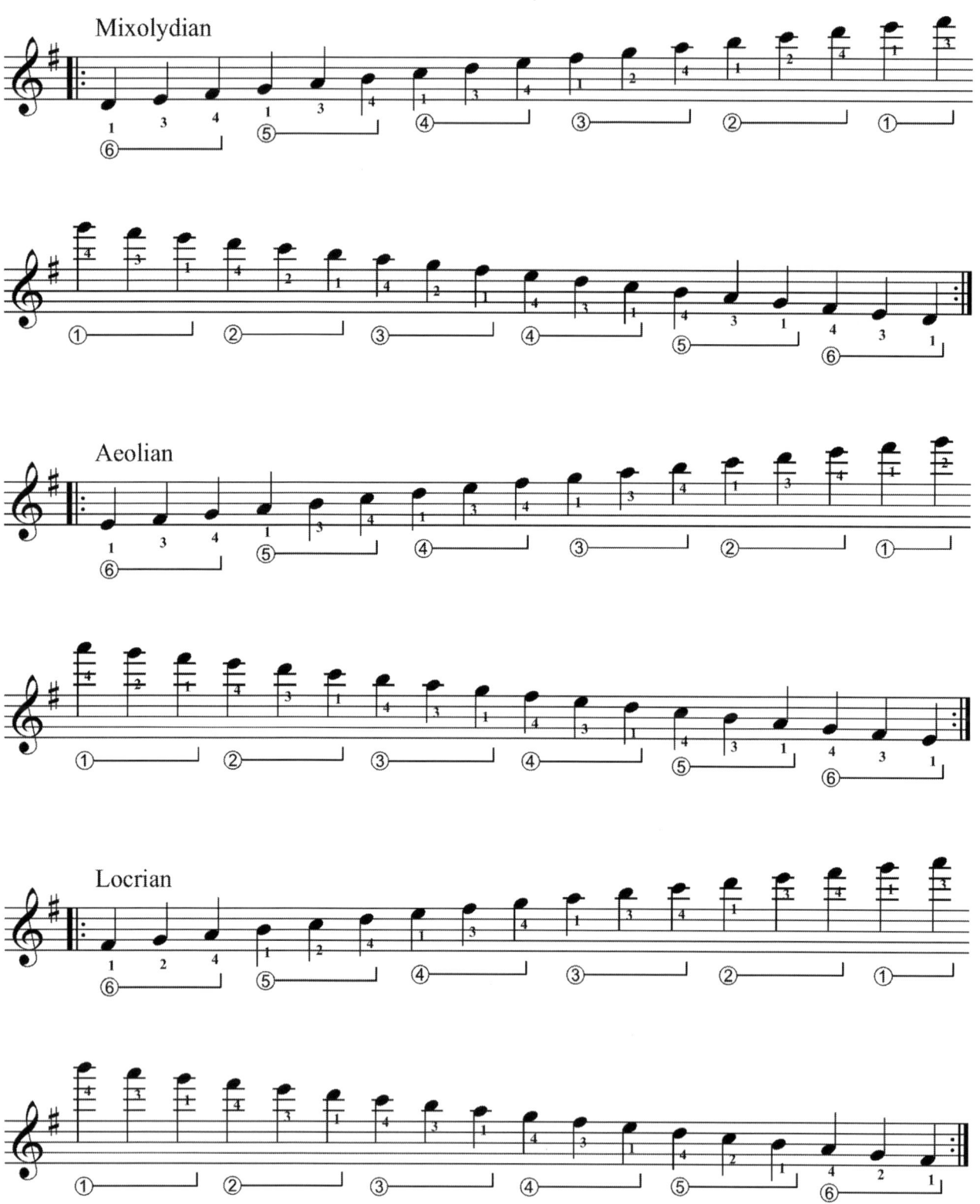

A Melodic Minor Positions

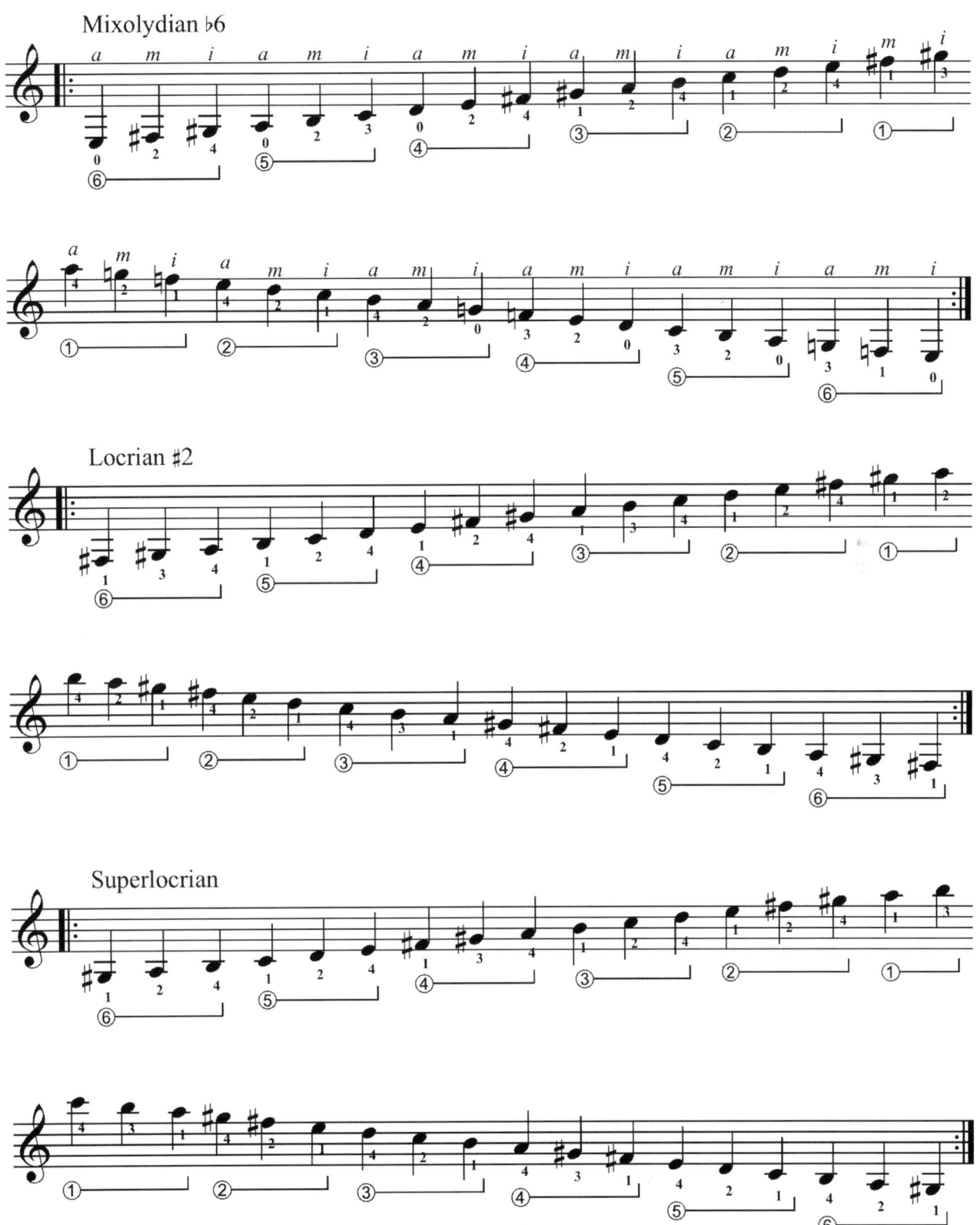

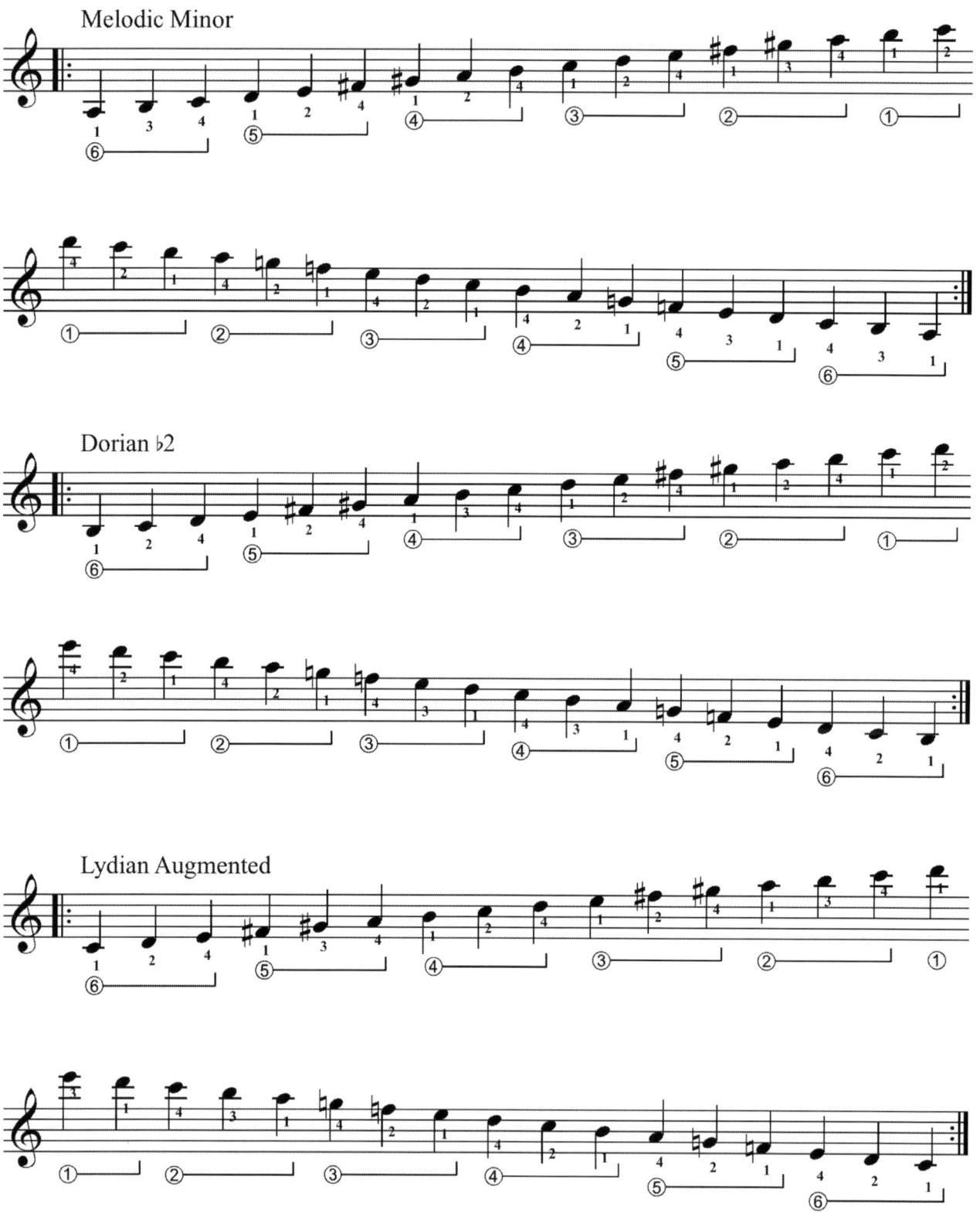

E Melodic Minor Positions

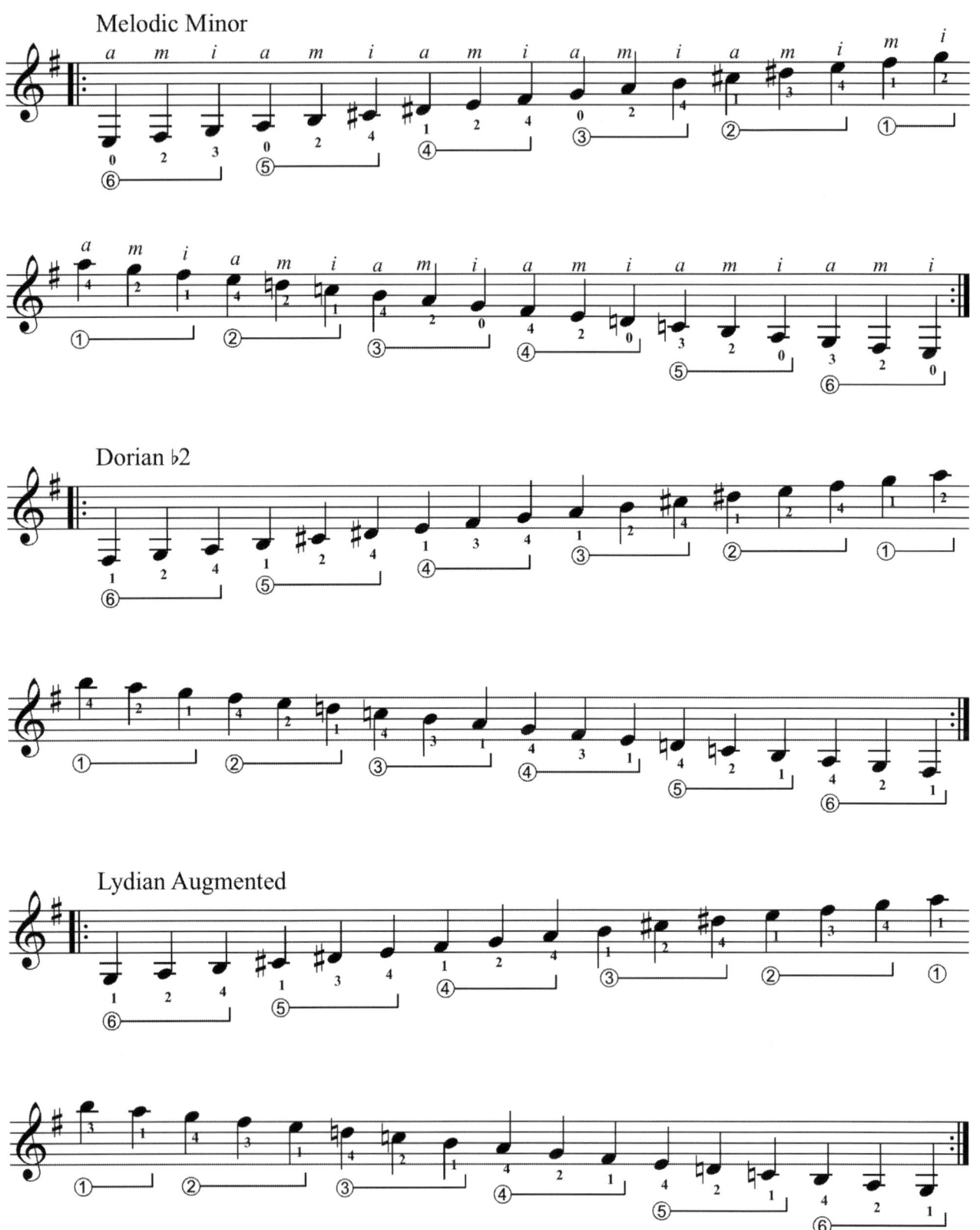

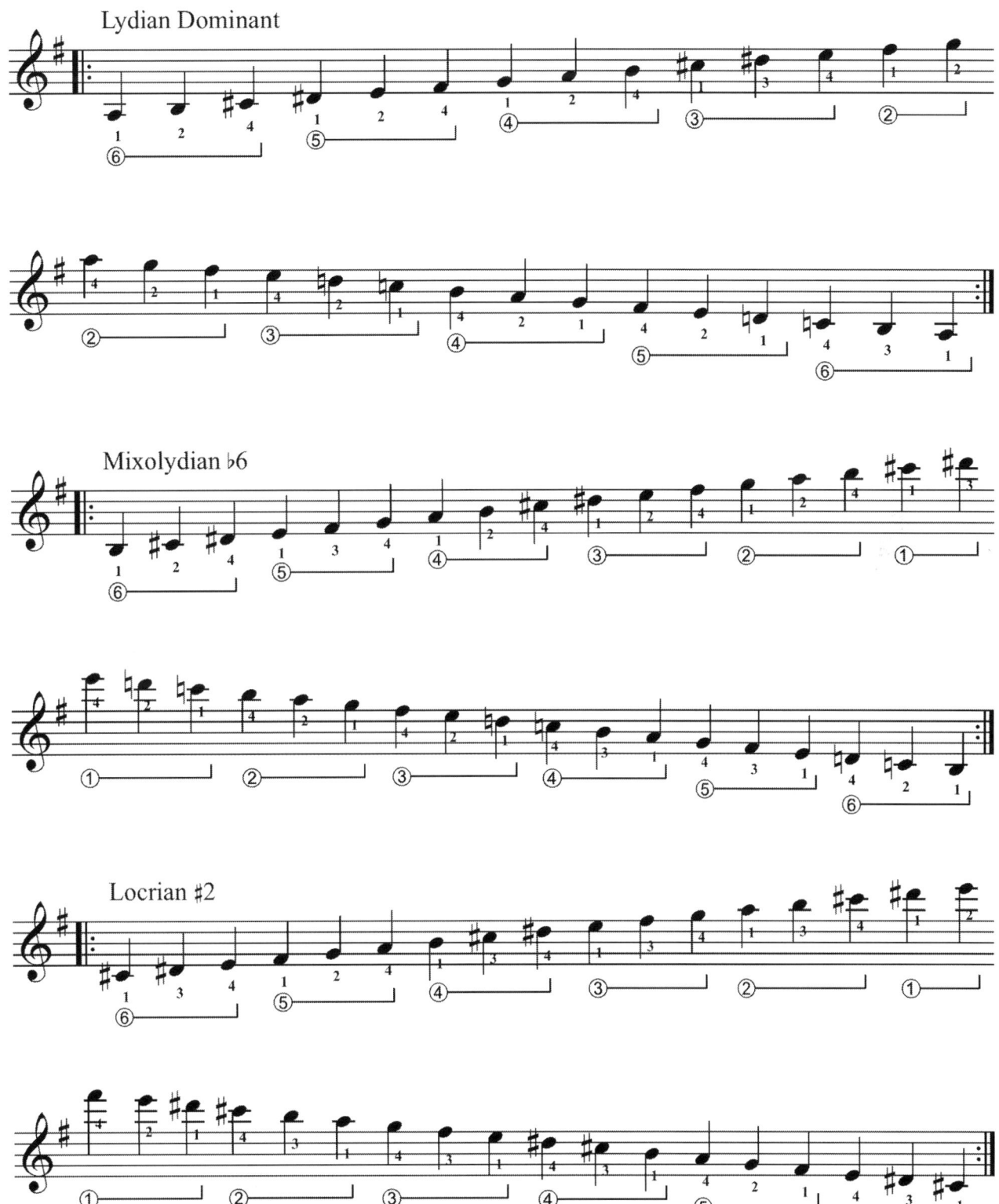

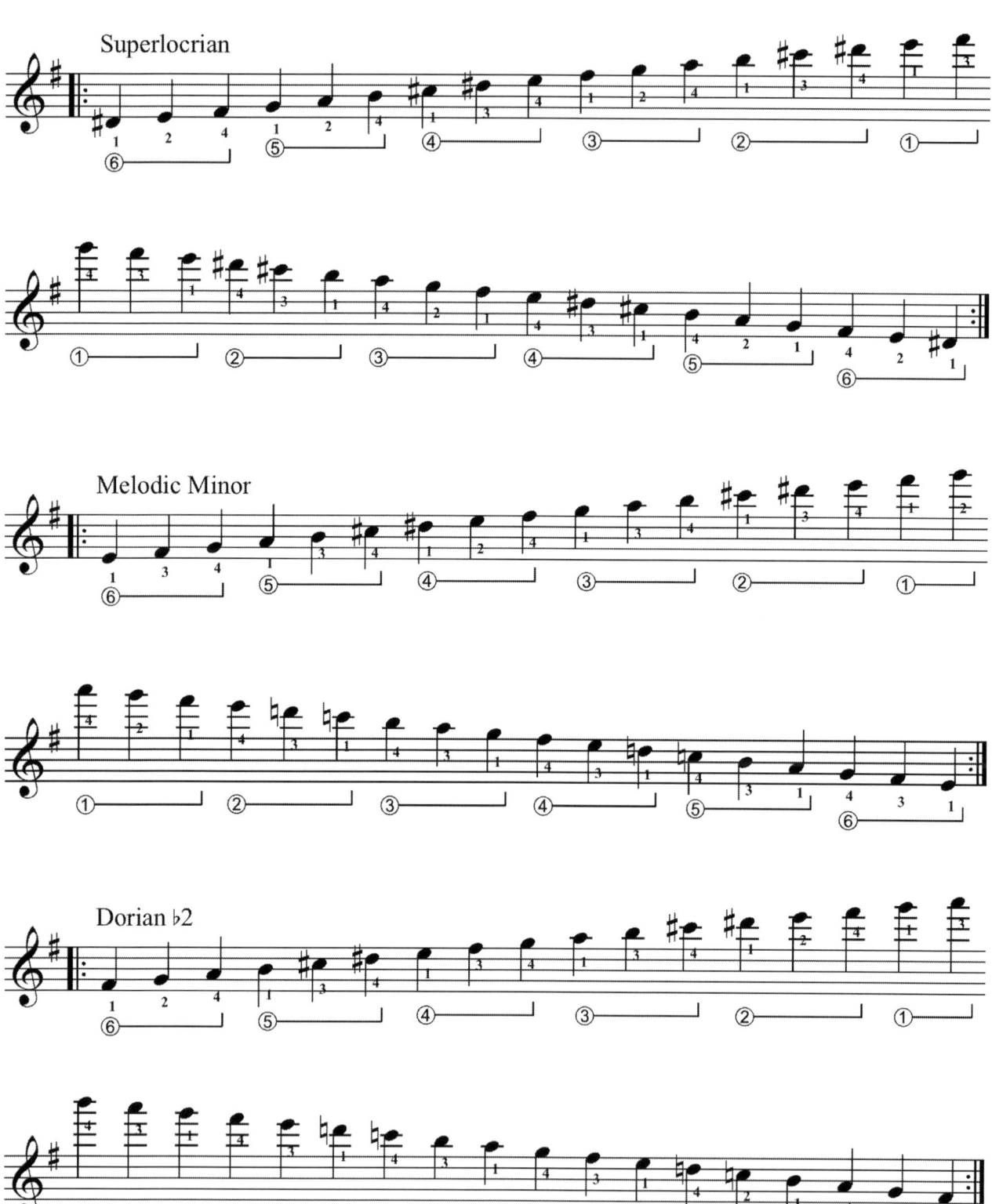

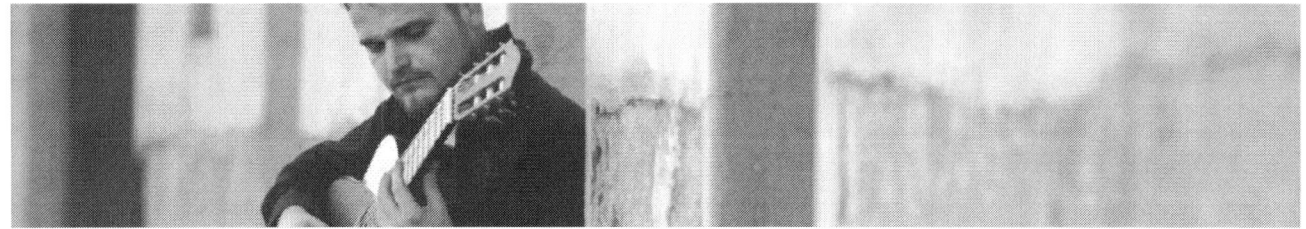

photo by Mamta Popat, Tucson, AZ

Guitarist Matt Palmer has appeared as a soloist throughout the United States, Europe, Mexico, Canada, South America, and the Caribbean. A recent recipient of the "Up and Coming Guitarist of the Year" award by *Guitar International Magazine*, Matt has been described by critics as "a young artist about to make a real dent in the world of classical guitar" *(Premier Guitar Magazine)*, "highly expressive and technically virtuosic" *(Modern Guitars Magazine)*, and "a truly accomplished and refined musician" *(Cleveland Classical)*. An active performer, winner of numerous guitar competitions, and author of *The Virtuoso Guitarist* method, Matt Palmer has gained worldwide recognition as a virtuosic and soulful concert artist.

His debut CD, *Un tiempo fue Itálica famosa*, has been applauded by *Guitar International Magazine* as "an album of the highest quality…with flawless technique, deep levels of personal expression, and an artistic integrity that seems far too rare these days." *Classical Voice of North Carolina* proclaims Matt's "positively nuclear" debut displays "stunning precision and unwavering accuracy enclosed in a huge dynamic envelope." In addition, Matt's pioneering guitar method, *The Virtuoso Guitarist*, has been recognized as a valuable addition to guitar pedagogy, and "indispensable for any advanced guitarist or teacher to include in their library" *(Classical Guitar Review)*.

Matt Palmer holds the Doctor of Musical Arts degree from The University of Arizona, where he studied with Thomas Patterson and Artists-in-Residence David Russell, Sergio Assad, and Odair Assad. Self-taught as a youth, he began his formal studies at age 20 with William Yelverton at Middle Tennessee State University, and later received his M.M. at Appalachian State University, where he studied with Douglas James. In demand as a performer, Matt's recent concert engagements have taken him to numerous universities, guitar societies, and dozens of international guitar festivals throughout the world.

- www.mattpalmerguitar.com -